St&

The story of RAF Carnaby

Best wishes

Gayna Wallis

By Gayna Wallis
2015

ISBN:

978-0-9569321-6-7

This book is dedicated to:

RAF Station Carnaby and to all those who needed her assistance.

I would also like to dedicate my book to my Mum, Audrey Wallis, who died shortly before my book was published. She supported me in everything I did and I will always miss you.

Published by Nu-Age Print & Copy

289 Padiham Road, Burnley, Lancs. BB12 0HA

Contents

Acknowledgements

Introduction

Chapter 1 A Brief History

Chapter 2 Emergency Runway - At all cost

Chapter 3 Fire, Fog and FIDO

Chapter 4 Lame Ducks and Diversions

Chapter 5 617 Squadron and the Grand Slam Bombs

Chapter 6 Friends and Allies

Chapter 7 Over paid, over sexed and over here!

Chapter 8 The Post War Years

Appendix – Roll of Honour

References

Acknowledgements

It would not have been possible to write this book without the help of so many kind people, willing to talk to me, giving me guidance and sharing their war-time memories with me. Firstly, I would like to thank John Larder and Sandrine Bauchet from the Yorkshire Air Museum for providing me with such great archive material about the Free French Air Force squadrons, aircraft crashes in Yorkshire, and for answering all my numerous questions, Peter Elliott from the RAF Museum for providing information about the RAF during WW2, The National Archives' staff for helping me with my research about Bomber Squadrons and for granting me permission to use their photos, Johnny Pye at Eden Camp, Imperial War Museums for their help with my research and providing me with a photo of F/Lt Checklin and his damaged aircraft, John Dann for giving me permission to use his photos, David Towers, Gerald Lilley and Sandy Wade for sharing their war-time memories with me, Rolph Walker, Curator of 158 Squadron, for helping to set straight the true record of F/Lt Checklin's story, Louise Bush of Lincolnshire Aviation Museum for providing me information about crashes and emergency landings, library staff at Bridlington and Beverley, Bourne Francis and Archie from 8th Airforce Historical Society for helping me with local research, and to Diana and Judith Redhead for proof reading my manuscript and to Doris Cairns for helping me find a publisher.

FIDO

Through the mist and rain

Through fog and flame

I will guide you home

Over land and sea

Through flak and fear

I will guide you home.

Introduction

In January 2014, a few local residents of Carnaby formed a committee called Carnaby Airfield Memorial (CAM). The aim of which is to raise funds for a memorial to be erected on the former airfield. This airfield was used as an Emergency Runway during World War 2 and helped to save many lives.

CAM recently obtained charity status on the 10th April 2015. To help raise funds I have researched the history of the airfield so that its contribution and the personal sacrifices that were made are not lost and forgotten by future generations. All monies raised by the sale of this book will go towards erecting a memorial to honour those that worked, served and landed here.

All facts in this book have been researched from the National Archives held at Kew, local and national air museums, and other published works. Some individuals have come forward and offered to tell of their personal stories and memories. I hope that I do them justice by re-telling their stories accurately. Some historical data has been difficult to obtain because the records have either become lost or destroyed over time. In particular, obtaining records from the USAAF have proved the most futile, and many of the USAAF aircrew names remain incomplete.

I have tried, where possible, to record a "roll of honour" of all the service personnel that worked, landed or served at RAF Station Carnaby during WW2. My research is still ongoing and there are many more Squadrons to research.

I hope that you enjoy reading this book. If you would like to know more about CAM please visit our website www.carnabyairfieldmemorial.org. Registered Charity Number 1161231. Thank you.

Gayna Wallis

Chapter 1
A Brief History

Events leading up to World War 2 are well known and widely published. What perhaps is not so well known is how and why small airfields, like Carnaby, were established in the first place. Some of these WW2 airfields have now fallen into disuse or disrepair, and others, such as Carnaby, have been regenerated into small, thriving industrial estates. Often we drive past them with little or no thought as to what was once a significant undertaking. The sacrifices that each and every airfield made now lie buried and mostly forgotten, except by a few, they are ghosts of the past and lost to the realms of history.

To fully appreciate the significance that these airfields made in Britain, it is fundamental to understand why they were created in the first place. We therefore start with a brief introduction about the events that led up to their conception.

After the First World War international conventions were held to discuss the issue of warfare, and in particular aerial warfare. There was great concern that aerial warfare may be used in the future from aggressive nations, and therefore it was imperative that international agreements were secured. In the early 1920's, the Washington Conference held talks (Limitation of Armaments) about banning the bomber. The Hague Rules of Aerial Warfare believed that a military target was legitimate. However, it first had to be decided what constituted as a military target. After lengthy talks no such definition was ever ratified, leaving countries like Britain in fear of aerial bombardment. The rules of engagement of bombing "legal military targets" was now left to each individual country to decide. In 1932, the League of Nations resumed these talks but after a year of little progress Germany pulled out.

Britain kept a close eye on Europe and were soon alerted to the emergence of a strong new leader in Germany, Adolf Hitler. Hitler was steadily gaining power and strength, unsettling the British Government. It was not long before the British Government realised that Hitler was rearming Germany. This added to Britain's fear of aerial bombardment and deep concern grew about a weakness in her defences. Britain took decisive action and immediately increased aircraft production, focusing on the bomber. Bomber Squadrons also increased to well over 120. Initially, they were equipped with twin-engine bombers, such as Wellingtons, Whitleys and Hampdens. Bomber Command, which had recently formed, would take full control over these Squadrons.

In 1935, the RAF's Expansion Scheme planned to build 100 new military airfields in Britain to cope with the increase in Bomber Squadrons. Evidence was mounting that Germany was a likely threat, therefore it was imperative that bombers reached Berlin in the shortest possible time. Latitudinally, the counties of Yorkshire and Lincolnshire lay on the most direct route and so within months, airfields began to spread across these counties, earning them the name of "Bomber Counties".

In 1936, the East Riding of Yorkshire saw the creation of two new permanent RAF stations; RAF Driffield, and RAF Leconfield. Emergency airfields like Carnaby were not even a consideration at this time. It never occurred to the Air Ministry that Britain would need such a thing.

In September 1939, the unthinkable happened; Germany invaded Poland. As Britain had sworn to protect Poland against future aggressors following the First World War, the British Prime Minister, Neville Chamberlain, stepped in to aid Poland, giving an ultimatum to Germany to withdraw its troops immediately. Germany did no such thing and with a heavy heart, Chamberlain made his famous speech to the public by wireless at 11.15 on the morning of the 3rd September 1939 stating:

"This morning the British Ambassador in Berlin handed the German Government a final Note stating that, unless we heard from them by 11 o'clock that they were prepared at once to withdraw their troops from Poland, a state of war would exist between us.

I have to tell you now that no such undertaking has been received and that consequently this country is at war with Germany."

Britain was plunged into the brink of war yet again, and took a heavy battering over the following months. By May 1940, Chamberlain had resigned from his post after being forced to retreat from Norway. He was succeeded by Winston Churchill who had considerable experience of warfare, and was therefore deemed to be the man to lead the country through another war. However, in the early days of Churchill's premiership Britain suffered appalling losses. The RAF bearing the brunt of those losses from the well-accomplished German Luftwaffe. Daylight raids by the RAF were disastrous as British bombers, easily identified, were shot down in their droves. Bomber Command had to rethink tactics and quickly changed to night flying instead. Unfortunately, little thought had been given to the aircrews who were unfamiliar with night flying. Their accuracy of hitting targets was poor and they continued to lose aircraft with a high casualty rate. Eventually, in 1941, Churchill stepped in and suspended bombing operations until a solution could be found.

Britain needed a new strategy. Bigger and faster bombers were needed and more aircrew were needed to fly them. Even though the Commonwealth countries were contributing to the war effort and providing trained aircrew it was still not enough to beat the power and tenacity of the Third Reich. Britain was desperate for the USA to step in, however, they had an Isolation Policy in place to keep them out of the war for as long as possible. Until then, Britain and her Empire had to fight on alone.

Britain stepped up her production of armaments, and put more effort into aircraft production, focusing on bigger and faster bombers. By the latter end of 1941, twin-engine bombers were being replaced with the much more powerful four-engine bombers, such as the Short-Stirling, the Handley-Page Halifax and the legendary Avro Lancaster.

Bomber Command was strengthened even further with a change of leadership. The dynamic new Commander-in-Chief, Air Marshall Sir Arthur "Bomber" Harris, took command and helped to change its fortunes too. Harris soon made an impact, quickly approving new radar technologies, such a "Gee, Oboe and H2S" to aid navigation, and extended air crew training from six weeks to ten weeks. Bombing accuracy also improved dramatically by the creation of the elite new "Pathfinder Force". However, Harris had initially opposed this as he felt a *"corps d'elite"* would lead to dissention among other Groups under his command. Fortunately, Harris was proved wrong on this occasion and the Pathfinders were invaluable to less experienced crews. Finally, Britain started to make headway.

The Pathfinder Force consisted of five squadrons manned by very experienced pilots and navigators. They were all volunteers who had survived and completed their obligatory 30 ops. They then volunteered to join the Pathfinders for another tour of duty for another 30 ops! Their objective was to fly ahead of the main task force and to identify the bombing target, they would then drop illuminated flares over it so that the main task force (and less experienced crews) following close behind would then bomb the target with greater accuracy.

Bomber Harris firmly believed that Germany could be bombed into submission. His plan was therefore to implement strategic bombing in the heart of Germany's industrial areas, targeting warfare production plants. The Casablanca Directive, which was drawn up in January 1943 by the Combined Chiefs of Staff, allowed him to carry out his carefully thought-out plans. The first wave of attacks on the Ruhr saw thirty-one raids, causing massive destruction but also resulted in a heavy loss of civilian lives. Likewise, Bomber Command suffered heavy losses too. A total of 1,045 aircraft were lost and more than 5,500 airmen were killed or missing during these raids.

Further heavy losses were sustained between August 1943 and March 1944 with the loss of more than 600 aircraft and 2,690 airmen. The heaviest single loss of the war occurred on the night of 30/31 March 1944 when 95 aircraft out of a total force of 795 failed to return after the bombing of Nuremburg. This one night saw carnage in the skies, when German night fighters shot down British Bombers in their hordes. Never had the RAF lost so many men and aircraft in just one single night. Many of these losses may well have been prevented but a combination of mistakes in planning and poor weather conditions proved fatal when they came up against the might of the German Luftwaffe. Not only was this catastrophic loss a devastating blow for Bomber Command but it badly affected the morale of Britain. Shocked by such losses the Air Ministry curtailed all bombing raids until they had a firm strategy in place to improve the safety for bombers. These kinds of losses were unsustainable and a solution had to be found.

One solution, which had been on the back burner for several months, came to the fore front once again. The Air Ministry had talked a great deal in the last few months about constructing more runways down the east coast of England. It was now imperative that action was taken to get construction underway. These runways would be known as Emergency Runways and would be used solely for badly damaged aircraft that were unlikely to make it back to their own home bases or for use in poor weather conditions.

Construction of these airfields started as early as 1942 but due to shortages of labour and sourcing of appropriate land made delays inevitable. As a consequence, some of these airfields, like RAF Carnaby were not operational until 1944. However, during its short existence, Carnaby made a substantial contribution in saving the lives of thousands of airmen that used it. It was fitted with a unique and secret installation, known simply as FIDO, which aided stricken bombers to land safely in poor weather conditions. Carnaby became well known to pilots and aircrew alike, however, its secret installation was a well-kept secret throughout the war.

This book tells the story of RAF Station Carnaby and the men that it saved and the men that saved Britain!

Chapter 2
Emergency Runway - at all cost

Photo printed with kind permission from The National Archives.

The development and construction of emergency runways was a costly and time-consuming business. The decision about where to build these runways was not an easy task and involved the cooperation of several Government departments, including the Ministry of Agriculture, the Air Ministry, and Bomber Command. Valuable agricultural lands were not favoured sites as food production was an absolute necessity as many merchant ships were being sunk in the Atlantic at an alarming rate. The Government therefore had to ensure that Britain could grow enough food to feed the nation or face inevitable starvation.

Discussions about constructing emergency runways began as early as October 1941 at Bomber Command HQ in High Wycombe. A proposal was put forward to construct a series of new runways in the east of England for use during adverse weather conditions and to counter enemy intruders. Each Group was asked to submit their requirements and to suggest suitable sites for these new runways. Group 4, whose headquarters were based in York, proposed the following: *(taken from Air 14/1610)*

"Length of runways should be two miles by 150 to 200 yards wide, and three runways should be provided at each site radiating from a central point used for disposal and control.

Three sites are suggested:-

    i.   On the Norfolk coast near Langham
    ii. On the Yorkshire coast near Catfoss or Hornsea
    iii. On high ground in East Riding of Yorkshire at COLD KIRBY

At the first two sites runways should be positioned as near sea level as poss. and in areas usually unaffected by fog, but when fog conditions exists COLD KIRBY at an altitude of 1,000ft would prove invaluable".

Headquarters of No 4 Group, Heslington Hall, near York (now part of the University of York).

Three sites in Yorkshire were initially proposed and considered but then subsequently disregarded. Carnaby was not even a possibility during these early discussions, it only became a consideration after these sites were found to be wanting. However, Carnaby was by no means a popular choice either. Bomber Command made several objections about Carnaby's suitability as an emergency runway. Their main objections were that Carnaby was not free from fog, had high ground to the north rising over the Wolds and onto the Moors, and was deemed to be too close to the town of Bridlington, posing a risk to the residents should bombers fall short of the runway. Bomber Command were not the only ones to put in an objection. Opposition was also received from the Ministries of Agriculture, and the War Transport Department, but after further deliberations with the Air Ministry, they subsequently withdrew their objections.

On the 7th October 1942, authorisation for the requisition of the site at Carnaby was formerly received and orders were given to prepare it as a Bomber Command Emergency Runway. Bomber Harris objected several times to Carnaby becoming an emergency runway. However, two weeks later on the 19th October, Air Chief Marshall, Sir C Courtney of the Air Ministry in London, wrote a letter to Bomber Harris advising him that Carnaby would now proceed despite his objections. The Air Ministry informed Harris that they had carefully considered his arguments against Carnaby (and Canterbury) but had overruled his objections because of the following factors:

(Taken from Air 14/1610)

   i.   *To attempt at this stage to find and clear alternative sites would entail a delay of at least four months. There is, moreover, no certainty that better locations can be found, particularly in the Kent area*

  ii. *A very considerable amount of time and effort has been expended in clearing these sites with other Government Departments*

 iii. *Although both sites (referring to Carnaby and Canterbury) are by no means perfect, their disadvantages cannot be considered sufficiently serious as to preclude their being used satisfactorily as Emergency Runways.*

Bomber Harris less than graciously accepted their decision and his written response to Courtney at being out ranked read:

"If this is the position we must make the best of it, and it only remains to get on with the work as quickly as possible. But it is no good getting something which does not answer the purpose."

The next dilemma for the Air Ministry was to find a name for the runway. Initially, it had been referred to as "BRIDLINGTON", but as there already was an Initial Training Wing (ITW) in the town of Bridlington it was deemed likely that this would lead to confusion, so the name "BRIDLINGTON" was dropped in favour of a more suitable option. The proposed site for the runway was actually on land known as Carnaby Moor, just half a mile south of the village of Carnaby. Running adjacent to the proposed site was a railway linking the town of Bridlington with the city of Hull (Kingston-Upon–Hull). The nearest railway stations were Carnaby and Burton Agnes and the nearest villages were Haisthorpe and Thornholme which were at the west end of the runway.

As the airfield was to be built on Carnaby Moor itself, this name was put forward as a possibility, however it was thought that some may confuse it with the airfield at Thornaby. The President of the Aerodromes Board (PAB) C Longstaff, disagreed stating that

> *"I like Carnaby without the MOOR. I don't think anyone can confuse the name Thornaby. If so "god help them!"*

Finally, work could now begin on constructing the airfield. However, there were some complications. The Ministry of War Transport objected to the closure of the road from Carnaby Station that ran southwards and over the eastern end of the runway. Consequently, the road remained opened throughout the war and was only closed when aircraft activity was expected. The road was closed between the hours of dawn and dusk every night to allow for bombers to land and occasionally closed during the day for late returning bombers. One local school boy, Sandy Wade, who lived south of the railway line, took full advantage of this by cycling home as fast as he could at lunchtimes before the bombers arrived, knowing full well that the road could soon be closed for returning bombers who were unable to reach their bases. Once the road was closed, returning to school for afternoon classes was out of the question. There was, of course, only one thing that a school boy could do, and that was to sit and watch the battle-damaged bombers make their emergency landings on the aerodrome. What a thrill! Well worth missing a few lessons for and the inevitable telling off for missing school!

Construction

The contract to build the runway was given to Messrs A Monk. However, before construction could commence a local woman, Miss Mary Kitson Clark, informed the Air Ministry that there was an ancient earthworks situated near Carnaby railway station. Concern was raised that this was an ancient site and may hold important antiquities. This posed a serious problem and a major delay to the Air Ministry who now had a duty to investigate this matter thoroughly. The Air Ministry arranged for the site to be scientifically examined by an archaeologist and to ascertain whether it did indeed hold any antiquities of significance before being destroyed. It took several weeks before the site could be excavated and examined thoroughly. Eventually, the archaeologist concluded his finding and presented them to the Air Ministry by the 23rd February 1943. His findings showed that the ancient earthworks contained flints and pottery dating back to the Bronze Age. Although these were significant findings, it was not significant enough to stop the construction of the airfield. It is not clear what happened to those antiquities after the dig but shortly afterwards construction of the new runway began.

Photos of the runway at Carnaby (permission granted from The National Archives)

The land on Carnaby Moor was fairly boggy ground, which created a problem when constructing the airfield. The runway needed a firm foundation of hard-core to provide a good base layer and then required two inches of slag dust on top, followed by ten inches of slag. This layer was then rolled into position by heavy steam rollers and then covered by a four-inch layer of thick sand mix, which was collected from the beach situated just a mile away. The surface of the runway was finally finished off with a layer of bitumen and then painted with the runway markings. Local farmer, Mr Wade, recalls that one of the steamrollers was so heavy it sank into the bog and was never recovered. It now lies somewhere underneath the old runway and has never been recovered.

The positioning of the new runway was very strategic. It was 7-8 miles southwest of Flamborough Head and pointed directly into the prevailing winds. The headland was, and still is, an exceedingly well-known and recognisable landmark. To give an unobstructed approach to the runway at Carnaby, some tree felling was needed. The runway was laid on a latitude of 54 degree 4 N and a longitude of 0 degree 16 W. This photograph shows a pilot's view of the

(Permission granted from The National Archives)

runway when coming in over the headland. The Bay of Bridlington lies to the left, and to the right, lie the Yorkshire Wolds. On a perfectly clear day, it was easy to see a safe landing place for battle-damaged bombers that were struggling to make it home.

The First Emergency Landings

The first emergency landings were made even before the airfield had been fully constructed, much to the surprise of the men still working on it! The following is an excerpt from the National Archives records AIR 24/286.

(Excerpts from AIR 24/286: permission granted to use photo from The National Archives).

"Even before the Emergency Runway at Carnaby was completed two aircraft made emergency landings one even made a belly landing. At the time of the landing the contractor's men were busily engaged on the runway. The Clerk of Works complained that the men had then threatened to volunteer service in the mines."

The actual date is not recorded but it appears to be at the end of February 1944. The details of these landings are not known as the Station's Operation book has no record of them. They were however mentioned in a bulletin by the Air-Vice Marshall of Bomber Command on the 1st March 1944 who then distributed it to each Group in Bomber Command. It warned all pilots about "the dangers of landing on runways that were still under construction." What was apparent from this incident was that emergency runways like Carnaby were very much in need. Had this runway not been there, these aircraft would probably have had to crash land in the vicinity, with possible loss of life.

Completion of the runway

In a few short weeks after the first emergency landings the runway was finally completed. Unlike most other airfields, Carnaby was a little different. It was wider and longer than most other runways, in fact, it was five times wider than other airfields. In total, it was 3,000 yards long, and had a width of 250 yards. It had three separate lanes 75 yards apart for landing or taking off. If needed, three heavy bombers could land simultaneously on the runway. There was a 500 yard grass undershoot area at the East end and a 500 yard grass overshoot at the West end. The landing lane was reserved for aircraft in need of immediate assistance and was enclosed between the white lines and the word "Emergency" painted in white 12 foot lettering across the width of the landing lane at both ends. At night, the runway was fitted with the standard lighting with three coloured channels, GREEN, WHITE and YELLOW in that order. Reading from the South, the GREEN lighted channel was for emergency landings only.

To assist pilots in identifying aerodromes special markers called aerial lighthouses and landmark beacons were positioned a few miles away. The aerial lighthouse for Carnaby was located in the West about three miles away, and the Landmark Beacon was sited in the South East, approximately five miles away. These markers were of great importance to pilots when approaching unfamiliar airfields, especially under the cover of darkness. To further assist with landing, special lighting called SANDRA lights illuminated the four corners of the runway.

One of the most important and top secret features installed on this runway was that of FIDO (Fog Investigation Dispersal Operation). FIDO was known as the fog buster. Pipelines were laid along the runway into which fuel was then pumped. During low visibility and fog, ground crew were ordered to light FIDO to give assistance to pilots who were struggling to find the airfield in poor weather conditions. Within minutes, on a full burn, the heat from the burning fuel would burn a hole in the fog. This "window" in the fog was often enough to enable a pilot to see the runway and make a safe landing. This feature alone, saved the lives of hundreds of men. Only three emergency runways were fitted with this equipment; the other two being Woodbridge and Manston.

A total of 12 airfields in England (including the three emergency runways) were also equipped with FIDO, making it a very rare commodity indeed. Thousands of gallons of fuel were needed to run it for just one hour and a constant supply of fuel was needed. Luckily, Carnaby was able to refuel very quickly and efficiently as the runway ran alongside the L.N.E.R. railway and an extra siding had been put in especially for this purpose.

Approximately half way down the runway, was the Control Tower. The Control Tower was type 343/43 and was placed in the centre of the runway to the south of the runway providing good views of both the East and West end of the runway. This was the centre of all operations at Carnaby. It was equipped with HF/DF radio aids, TR1196, DARKY, and SBA. It would later be fitted with more advanced technology in the form of VHF/DF and VHF/BA radios. On the left hand side of the Control Tower was the Aircrew Reception. This is where all aircrew signed in once they have landed safely so that their respective bases could be informed of their arrival and therefore make the appropriate arrangements to transport them back to their home bases.

There were no hangars at Carnaby in which to park stationary aircraft. Instead there were 46 hard standing areas at the west end of the runway, which were laid around a circular track. A further 27 hard standing areas were constructed further up the runway, these were used for aircraft that were still serviceable and manoeuvrable. For aircraft that were badly shot up or crashed on landing were quickly moved to a safer area of the aerodrome.

Carnaby was well equipped to deal with emergencies, it had twelve crash bays, and 25 yards wide, in which immobilised aircraft could be pushed or pulled out of the way and in some cases even scrapped. A dispersal loop 420 yards in diameter was constructed at the west end of the runway to facilitate landings, and take-offs and traffic were circulated in a clockwise direction. Unfortunately, it was built on a gradient of 1:50 uphill on the first leg, then downhill on the rest, making it difficult for aircraft to manoeuvre easily, especially for those with brake problems. During the first early weeks several incidents occurred on the dispersal loop because of this fault. A new protocol was then put in place instructing crews that any aircraft with brake problems should be towed away instead.

To assist pilots in landing safely on airfields, the Air Ministry issued procedures for take-offs and landings. Below is an excerpt from Air 14/1610 for the procedure for Carnaby.

FLYING CONTROL PROCEDURE FOR CARNABY

Procedure when it is imperative that aircraft land immediately e.g lack of petrol etc

   i.   *Pilots are to approach the airfield from the East flying on the E-W line of approach, with navigation lights on.*

   ii. *Pilots are not to circle the beacon or the aerodrome, but are to come straight in on a long approach, through the funnel and land on the Red flare path. If possible Control should be contacted on R/T and informed of the approach.*

   iii. *On the approach to the funnel pilots are to indicate distress by switching the landing light and/or navigation lights on and off for short periods. This should be continued until the main funnel is passed.*

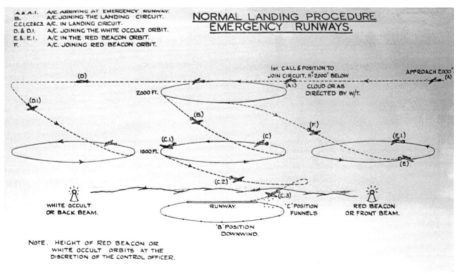

(Permission granted from The National Archives)

It was not just damaged aircraft that Carnaby could deal with efficiently. It could also deal with injured airmen. Carnaby had its own hospital or Sick Quarters, which were built just to the south of the runway, on the corner of Moor Lane/Sticks Lane. It also had its own mortuary as well.

Defence

Security at Carnaby was high and was defended by 1 AA Squadron, RAF Regiment. They were armed with 4 Borfors, 16 Hispano Guns, and approximately 300 personnel armed with rifles, Sten Guns and 8 pairs of Browning AA Guns. Around the airfield, there were 8 areas which were heavily defended by AA Weapons, each manned by one flight of 30 personnel.

Crash Party

When an aircraft was expected to land at Carnaby two airfield controllers were required – one at the East end of the Runway (A) and one at the West end of the overshoot (B). They were housed in a small hut with windows giving a clear view to East, North and West with a telephone and T/R receiver. Each Airfield Controller had a lorry carrying a large number of Red Glims and Hurricane lamps complete with a driver and one assistant. The Airfield Controllers were forbidden to leave their telephone without permission from the Control Office.

In the event of the runway becoming totally unserviceable, Airfield Controller (A) would fire red verey lights (with Control Officer Permission) to warn other approaching aircraft that no more landings were possible. Airfield Controller (B) would then layout two Glim light Flarepaths on the overshoot and would exercise control of the belly landing area. He would then operate Chance lights or SANDRA lights to light up the overshoot area.

Each airfield had its own Crash Crew. Carnaby's Crash Crew was manned by 43 Group. The Crash Crew were responsible for the removal and salvage of damaged aircraft on the runway. It was imperative they moved quickly and efficiently in order to clear the runway of any damaged aircraft before it was needed for the next emergency landing. Crash and fire tenders were on constant standby and were housed on the hard-standing at the dispersal point to the east of the Control Tower. The Ambulance Party would work under the immediate control of the Medical Officer and had to be well-acquainted with the layout of the runway and the procedures for its use.

When it was known that a crash landing would occur on the overshoot, both the Crash and Fire Tenders had to proceed to the West end of the Runway and wait to the left of the Glim Flarepath. Once the aircraft had touched down both these parties would then chase the distressed aircraft to its landing spot and give immediate assistance. A Reserve Fire Tender and Crew would then be in readiness as soon as No 1 Crew moved off the runway. Both Crash and Fire Crews had to use the M/T road when proceeding to a crashed aircraft for safety reasons. The Crash Crew was also responsible for making a thorough survey of the runway after a crash and remove all obstructions or debris before claiming that all landing paths were clear. Any damage to the runway was to be reported so that other lanes could be used instead. Any stranded aircraft on the runway would be towed away by the Tractor Crew upon direct orders from the Control Tower. A large 60ft trailer, known as a "Queen Mary" would take away any large debris such as wings or fuselage off the runway.

Gerald Lilley served in the RAF as a Sergeant just after the war. For a short period of time he was based at Driffield as part of a Crash Crew and occasionally had to attend crashes at Carnaby. He recalls driving a Watifer which was a two rear-axled Austin Fire Tender to several crashes at Carnaby. The Watifer, or Wati as it was often shortened to, was fitted with a 500 gallon water tank complete with a hose and jet gun. Any aircraft that was on fire was quickly doused with water by the driver of the Wati. They would also assist in getting aircrew off the bombers as quickly as possible. Two Austin Ambulances (with a driver and a medic on board) would also attend the crash and give urgent medical assistance if needed and would then transport any injured men to the hospital. A U/S Jeep and a CO_2 gas tender made up the rest of the Crash Party. The CO_2 gas tender was used to put out any electrical fires.

Gerald Lilley driving a Watifer as part of a crash crew when he was in the desert. This is the same type that was used at Carnaby.

Crash Crew were permanently on standby waiting for the next emergency to arrive. When an aircraft needed assistance the Crash Party had to wait until the order was given to attend. They would then race down the runway after the aircraft and give immediate aid. The Crash Party at Carnaby worked very quickly and efficiently and could clear the runway of damaged aircraft remarkably quickly, usually within minutes of the aircraft landing.

Gerald Lilley with an Austin ambulance

Once the aircrews had alighted from the aircraft they would then be directed to the Reception Hut. The Captain or pilot would then complete an "Aircraft Arrival Report" giving details of their aircraft, aircraft number, crew's name, ranks, squadron details, details of their sortie/target, damage to aircraft, details of casualties and the reason for landing at Carnaby. This information would then be used to contact the aircrews' home base and where possible, transport home would be arranged. If the crew's base was too far away they would be accommodated to the nearest RAF base at RAF Lissett for the night. However, there were times were even RAF Lissett could not accommodate aircrews, especially during large diversions.

Carnaby, being designated as an emergency runway only, was not equipped to accommodate arriving aircrews, hence the need for transporting them to Lissett. The camp at Carnaby, which was on the south side of the runway, only had enough accommodation to house its own ground staff, the maximum being 550, and had a communal area for personnel. The staff at Carnaby consisted of a total of 548 personnel - 18 officers, 36 SNCOs and 494 other ranks.

As Carnaby was so close to the sea aircraft often had to ditch into the North Sea if they were unable to reach the safety of the airfield. To accommodate the need to rescue ditched aircrew Bridlington was equipped with its own air-sea rescue unit. It patrolled a large area along the east coast, with the next nearest air-sea rescue unit being in Grimsby. In the event of an aircraft being known to have "ditched" or on the point of coming down on or near the sea, the Control Officer at Carnaby had to inform these units immediately stating that words *"Priority 1: Rescue Aircraft"*. These rescue crafts would then be launched with all speed.

Official Opening

On the 12th March 1944, the HQ of 4 Group received a secret memo from Bomber Command informing them that RAF Station Carnaby would be officially open as from the 16th March 1944; however, the station's record book shows that Carnaby actually opened on the 26th March 1944. The parent station was RAF Station Driffield which was responsible for pay, equipment and barracking arrangements. The official address and telephone details were as follows:

Telephone number for RAF Station Carnaby:

BRIDLINGTON 2408

Nearest railway station for passenger and goods was:

CARNABY L.N.E.R. (adjourning)

Official address:

R.A.F. Station
Carnaby
Bridlington, Yorks

Carnaby finally became fully operational on the 20th April 1944 and was designated the code name **"Station XI"**. This is quite astonishing given that the preceding code name, Station X, belonged to none other than Bletchley Park!

Chapter 3
Fog, Fire and FIDO

The history and development of FIDO is an interesting one and is well explained in Williams (1995) book "Flying through Fire". It gives a detailed account of how FIDO was developed and facts about each airfield that had it installed. This chapter will therefore give a brief summary of the research carried out by Williams and will also provide facts obtained from the records at the National Archives about the FIDO equipment that was installed at RAF Carnaby. It also highlights how and why the Government ordered the installation of very expensive and potentially dangerous equipment on only 12 airfields in England. RAF Carnaby being one of them.

Heavy operational losses early on in the war were beginning to take their toll on Bomber Command. It was not just losses through enemy action that were to blame but also crashes on returning to bases, training casualties and poor weather conditions. Fog was a major contributory factor for loss of aircraft and aircrew. In October 1940, fourteen aircraft (10 Hampdens and 4 Wellingtons) crashed when attempting to land at their bases in foggy conditions. This incident did not go unnoticed by Churchill and his War Cabinet. Churchill enquired about the arrangements that were in place for "blind landings" but did not receive an immediate answer. Fortunately, there was a perfectly good solution available albeit an expensive one.

Prior to the war, a Professor from Imperial College, London, David Brunt, calculated that fog could be cleared from airfields if the air temperature was raised by approximately 5°F. Dr J D Main-Smith and A S Hartshorn then carried out trials between 1936 and 1939 with trays of smokeless liquid fuel arranged in lines. The fuel was then set alight under foggy conditions and studied as to its efficacy in dispersing fog. These early trials proved that fog would evaporate if enough heat could be generated, however, it would need a lot of fuel to burn off substantial fog and would be deemed very costly. Having proved that this could be achieved, the trials were then shelved (Williams, 1995).

It took many more losses before the powers that be were to resurrect the old idea of burning off fog from airfields again. On 2nd September 1942, the Committee for the Co-ordination of the Bomber Offensive were asked for their recommendations. They recommended that the Air Minister for Supply and Organization (AMSO) and the Petroleum Warfare Department (PWD) undertake full scale trials in fog dispersal again. After several consultations the Air Minister, Sir Archibald Sinclair, wrote to Winston Churchill asking for his approval to restart these trials. Within 24 hours the Minister for Petroleum, Mr Geoffrey Lloyd, had received a personal memo from Churchill ordering him to resume these trials with immediate effect.

Trials began in earnest in October 1942. Initially, these trials were called "fog dispersal provisional investigation plan", which was then changed to "fog dispersal investigation operation" as it was easier to say. It was then changed to read "FIDO" for ease of tongue. At some point at the end of the war the wording was changed again to read "Fog, Intensive Dispersal Of" to conform to RAF jargon.

Full scale trials were carried out and adjustments to designs of burners were made. The Anglo-Iranian Oil Co provided the expertise in developing these burners, and so the first burners were named Haigas. The name Haigas was derived in part from the last initial of the Chief Engineer (Mr Hartley) and part of the initials of the company for whom he worked, (Anglo-Iranian Oil Co). The burners burnt petrol in the form of gas and so the word "gas" was used to complete the name. They were also known as Mk 1 burners.

A year earlier, proposals were put forward to construct emergency runways for battle-damaged aircraft returning from their missions. Three sites were finally identified; Woodbridge, Manston and Carnaby. The construction of the airfield at Carnaby began in 1943 and was completed in 1944, becoming fully operational in the April of that year. All three emergency runways were to be equipped with the top secret FIDO equipment with very tight security to ensure it remained a secret throughout the war.

The FIDO equipment consisted of a double row of Haigill Mk IV burners. These ran the length of the runway for approximately 2,000 yards on each side. Across the runway was another set of double burners and a Rapex burner was installed as well. In total, more than 180 Mk IV burners were installed along the runway and over 30,000 feet of piping was used.

If a full burn was needed it could use up a staggering 120,000 gallons of petrol per hour. The storage tanks had to hold enough fuel to enable the burners to burn on maximum output for six continuous hours. That is 720,000 gallons of fuel stored in tanks at just one airfield at any one time, just to be burned. It took 60 men to operate the valves on a full burn. FIDO was used approximately 250 times during the war and by December 1944, the burners had exceeded their lifespan by 100% and needed to be replaced, however, this was a four-week job. December was also proving to be a difficult month for the Station as the number of crew operating FIDO had been reduced to 19 men to operate 60 pits. Each valve needed to be manned, especially if an aircraft landed near one of the burners. This was far from ideal and greatly concerned the Station Commander.

Haigill burners were a modified and much improved version of the Haigas burners. Frank Gill was the Engineer who re-designed them and in his honour the burners were named Haigill. A further set of double row burners was also laid across the runway at Carnaby and a RAPEX (RAPidly EXtingusihed) burner was laid in a trench about a mile further down. RAPEX burners were much more powerful burners that were fitted with a vaporizer that could be rapidly extinguished. It was used on wider emergency runways, such as Carnaby. Many pilots disliked the idea of landing on a runway with a flame of fire across their path, however, they were very grateful for it when they needed to use it.

The runway at Carnaby ran alongside the LNER railway which had its own station until 1970. A special siding was built so that the much needed fuel could be brought in quickly to refuel FIDO. The first practice burn was held on the 19th July 1944 and was attended by a senior Meteorologist Sqn Ld Harry Edge, from PWD. The flare was so bright that the Fire Brigade in Bridlington were called. One local farmer still remembers FIDO being lighted and said it was so bright you could read a newspaper by its flame.

Carnaby was fitted with two pumphouses, which were equipped with Ford V8 engines that powered six Sulzer pumps. These pumps could pump around 500 gallons/min of fuel at a pressure of 90-100 lbs/sq inch if required, which is the equivalent of 240,000 gallons per hour. It took approximately 3 minutes for the burners to become fully alight and in less than 5 minutes the runway was fully operational. August 1st 1944 saw the first operational burn when a Halifax III bomber from Driffield was diverted owing to weather conditions at its base. It landed at 23.30 hrs as FIDO was in the process of being lighted. Five more Halifax III's then made good their landing between 23.37 hrs and 23.54 hrs. Just after midnight (00.09hrs) two more Halifaxes landed with the aid of FIDO. The weather was recorded as being very bad and visibility very poor. At 00.28 hrs another aircraft was on its approach to the runway. Unfortunately, this aircraft struck a house chimney pot with its port outer engine but luckily recovered and made a safe landing, with its propeller missing and its engine on fire. Then two more Halifaxes landed making a total of 11 landings with the aid of FIDO in one single night. The Station's log book records this momentous night:

> "Without FIDO these landings would have been extremely hazardous, if at all possible, and all the pilots appreciated the valuable aid that FIDO had given them".

Other reports show that one Halifax approached from the west (instead of the east-west direction, which was the normal route), asked for permission to land because he was short of fuel but was told to join the other aircraft which was already in circuit. However, he ignored this and attempted to land but was on a direct collision course with an aircraft making an emergency landing from the other direction. Fortuitously, the pilot was able to open up his throttle enough to lift clear of the approaching aircraft and a disaster was narrowly averted.

These crews were returning from the Pas de Calais in which a force of 777 aircraft (385 Lancasters, 324 Halifaxes, 67 Mosquitoes, and 1 Lightning) were to attack numerous flying bomb sites. Only 79 of these aircraft were able to bomb their targets, the rest of the sorties were aborted, probably due to poor weather conditions. Sixty-five of these aircraft were Halifaxes from the Yorkshire based 4 Group. Their target was the Chapelle Notre Dame but visibility was so poor that the raid was abandoned before H-hour and the bombers had to return fully laden with their bombs still on board. The next recorded landing with the aid of FIDO was on the 20th September 1944 when a Lancaster X needed assistance in landing. The weather conditions in September were appalling.

The table below has been adapted from the original Station's Operations Book held at the National Archives in Kew. It shows all the recorded FIDO landings at Carnaby.

Table 1

Date	Time	Aircraft	Crew	Details
01.02.44	23.30 23.37 to 23.54	1 Halifax III 5 Halifax III		Diverted from Driffield -
02.08.44	00.09 00.28 00.32 01.05	2 Halifax 1 Halifax 1 Halifax 1 Halifax		- Struck house chimney pot – damaged prop/engine on fire - -
20.09.44	20.20	1 Lancaster		Normal landing with aid of FIDO
19.12.44	00.47 02.45	1 Halifax 1 Halifax		Hydraulics u/s Hydraulics u/s
22.12.44	02.24- 03.15 12.20- 14.10 21.35 22.08	6 Lancasters 1 Lancaster 13 Fortresses 1 Halifax 1 Lancaster		Landed on diversion No brakes From 428 USAAF all making safe landing Navigation u/s Short of fuel
24- 26 .12.44				(Possible FIDO landings) Details unknown
29.12.44	12.58- 18.08	9 Halifaxes 1 Lancaster		Emergency landings with FIDO Emergency landings with FIDO
01.01.45	06.02- 07.35 13.08- .16.08	6 Stirlings 2 Halifaxes 1 Lancaster 1 Oxford		From 38 Group
23.01.45	00.47- 01.20	4 Halifaxes		Landed in thick mist, one Halifax made a 3 engined landing
31.01.45	10.32	65 Liberators 6 Halifaxes		Thick mist, all aircraft this day landed with aid of FIDO, many aircraft had varying faults
08.02.45	21.15	1 Lancaster		Of 1 Group, navigational aids u/s
15.02.45	09.38- 09.43	2 Fortresses		Diverted from 92 Group – FIDO assisted landing
22.02.45	13.08	1 Halifax		Undercarriage u/s, made a belly landing assisted by FIDO
25.02.45	18.37- 19.42	3 Halifaxes		Diverted from their bases owing to weather
12.03.45	12.26- 19.31	2 Lancasters 3 Halifaxes		1 x Undercarriage trouble, 1 x 3 engine landing 2 x brakeless landing, 1 x aileron u/s

Date	Time	Aircraft	Crew	Details
09.04.45	01.23-06.20	24 Halifaxes	F/Lt Ronald Lawson Sgt Frank Smith	Diverted, most with minor troubles, last one badly damaged over target area from photoflash inside the plane. Hole in floor, rear-gunner was thrown or fell through. Fortunately, his harness caught on a projection and he was brought back from Norway suspended beneath the plane. He made a remarkable recovery after 48 hours in SSQ

The last entry from the above table, dated 9th April 1945, clearly shows the dangers that aircrew faced on a nightly basis and how one's fate lies in the balance. The unfortunate rear-gunner who fell through the floor of his Halifax III was WOP/AG Sergeant Frank Smith of No 58 Squadron. Skipper F/Lt Ronald Lawson was returning to his base at Linton on Ouse, when the incident occurred. They had just bombed a merchant ship off the Norwegian coast. Their last 500lb bomb scored a direct hit amid ships and the flames could still be seen when they were 20-25 miles away. They attempted to photograph their target but the photoflash became detached from the carrier and was caught up in the lanyards from the flares released, unbeknown to the crew. When it was released it caused an explosion which tore a gaping hole in the fuselage of the Halifax. Such was the damage to the aircraft that airspeed was reduced. Lawson also discovered that one of his crew members were missing but had assumed that he had fallen through the hole and was now lost. Due to loss of airspeed and lack of fuel, Lawson changed his course and headed for Carnaby.

When they reached Carnaby it was shrouded in fog and they were asked to go elsewhere. However, due to fuel gauges on zero, Lawson had little choice in the matter and asked for immediate assistance. The Control Tower relented and gave the order for FIDO to be lit. The Halifax approached at a speed of 140 knots with no flaps to aid braking, and with flames on both sides from the FIDO pipes, they made a safe landing, braking hard. The flames died on landing and the crew sat for a few minutes lost in heavy fog. When they descended from their aircraft they discovered that their missing crew member, Sgt Smith, was still with them. His parachute harness had caught on a projection from the bomb bay and he had been suspended under the aircraft. His arms and legs were wrapped around damaged fuselage spars. He was still wearing his oxygen mask which saved his face from serious injury as he was dragged along the runway. His ordeal had lasted over three hours in freezing conditions over the North Sea. He was apparently still smiling when they released him. He spent the next 48 hours in the Station's Sick Quarters, making a full recovery before returning to ops.

Table 2. Adapted from AIR 27/545 Log Book Details of 58 Squadron – National Archives

Date	Aircraft Type & number	Crew	Duty	Time Up	Time Down	Details of sortie
08.04.45	Halifax PN 425 (E)	F/Lt R N Lawson F/Sgt J Ricketts P/O C H Kohler (Aus) F/Sgt W L Magness W/O R E Blades F/SGt FC Yeandle F/Sgt W Smith F/Sgt J F Smith F/O V Jones	A/S Patrol L 6	21.15	06.20	02.58 hours attacked in position 5848N-09.40 E a cargo type passenger M/V of approximately 3,000 tons, releasing 7x500lb MC bombs from 3,800 feet. The last bomb scored a direct hit, causing a cloud of smoke from forward of amid-ships. Flames could still be seen when aircraft was 20-25 miles away. No flak was experienced. Photography was attempted but the photoflash became detached from the carrier and was caught up in the lanyards from the flares released, unbeknown to the crew – so when released it exploded, causing extensive damage to the aircraft to such an extent that the air-speed was reduced and due to lack of fuel, Captain set course for Carnaby. It was revealed that after the aircraft landed that the mid-upper gunner had been blown out of the aircraft and was found to be hanging by his parachute harness to the jagged parts of

With so many aircraft landing at Carnaby it was increasingly difficult to accommodate and feed all the aircrews. Many were taken to RAF Lissett but this was also becoming over-crowded. Crews often had to wait several hours before being fed and housed after returning from sorties. This was now becoming unacceptable and the Station Commander continued to complain about the inadequacy of Carnaby's ability to cope with such huge diversions. He logged his concerns in the Station's log book. Some crews, fed up of waiting to be housed, even made their own way into the town of Bridlington to find more amenable accommodation and good food.

Chapter 4
Lame Ducks and Diversions

The dangers that pilots and aircrews faced on a daily basis must have been truly daunting. Most of us pale at the thought of flying through turbulence for just a few minutes! Yet, these courageous, young men braved the rigors and hardships of flying into battle day after day. Often caught up in intense flak which must have been more frightening than any turbulence we have ever experienced, not knowing if they would make it through the night. Aircrews were often pursued by enemy fighters and constantly bombarded with rapid bursts of fire, damaging the very structure that kept them airborne.

Bombers took a heavy battering during these encounters, often damaging some important electrical or mechanical equipment. Many an aircraft was known to have a missing propeller, loss of brake power, or an undercarriage that would not drop down. Fuselages would often have gaping holes in them, tyres would burst on impact or some vital navigation component would be shot to pieces. Despite this, aircrews would continue on regardless of their own safety, some would have had no choice, others choosing to carry on and complete their bombing mission before turning for home. They would turn their "lame duck" homewards praying they had enough luck and fuel to get them home.

Carnaby saw many a "lame duck" winging its precarious way back to the airfield to make an emergency landing. Many had undercarriage problems and had to land either with wheels unlocked, one wheel down or no wheels at all! Belly landings were commonplace and most made it down safely. Carnaby coped with them all. Crash crews were quick to respond and could clear the runway within minutes of a touchdown. Even if one lane was blocked, there were still two more lanes available to use. This made Carnaby one of the safest landing grounds in the country with few fatalities. The skill and strength needed to land these shot-up bombers is truly remarkable and is to be greatly admired even by today's standards.

For a small RAF Station, Carnaby was able to deal with all that was thrown at it. The Crash Crews were well trained with a strict procedure in place to deal with all emergencies. The Crash Crew at Carnaby consisted of two Austin Ambulances with a driver and medic on board: a Fire Tender (Watifer) which was a two-axled vehicle with a 500 gallon water tank, hose and a jet gun; a US jeep and a CO_2 gas tender. They were based just to the left of the Control Tower and were ready to move at a moment's notice when the Control Tower gave the command. They were not allowed to drive down the runway itself but had to use a road parallel to it. This was to avoid collisions with incoming aircraft and had to be adhered to no matter what.

Once the Crash Crews had put the fires out and the medics had attended to the injured, any aircraft that could not be taxied off the runway had to be removed quickly. Aircraft were usually towed away by tractors but any completely wrecked aircraft were moved by a 60ft trailer pulled by a tractor, known colloquially as a "Queen Mary". Salvage teams would collect the debris and search the runway for any aircraft parts that had become dislodged during the landing. All debris had to be removed quickly and as efficiently as possible to prevent accidents occurring upon landing. Damaged aircraft were given categories according to their airworthiness (A, AC, C, E and E2). Those that were not badly damaged were repaired but some were totally smashed and their parts used for spares.

It was not just battle-damaged aircraft that used Carnaby. Many aircraft were also diverted here because of poor weather conditions. With the FIDO installation at Carnaby aircraft could land in all weather conditions. Some diversion were extremely large and totally inundated the meagre facilities at Carnaby. During these occasions, the runway would be stacked up with stationary aircraft, and accommodation, always at a premium, outstripped demand by far, often causing concern to the Station Commander.

It was not just bombers that landed at Carnaby, the occasional fighter would also require assistance. Carnaby also played host to a wide range of nationalities, including the Australians, New Zealanders, Canadians, Americans and the Free French Air Force. All were grateful for the assistance that Carnaby gave.

It is therefore befitting that some of their remarkable stories and sorties are retold, lest we forget. These are just a few accounts of how these young aircrews brought their "lame ducks" home on a wing and a prayer.

Lame Ducks

18th July 1944- Excerpts from Air 24/286 National Archives, Kew.

"Carnaby proved its ability to deal well with "lame ducks". On the 18th July 1944 when aircraft were returning from an attack on the battlefront in Normandy Carnaby had to deal with two emergencies. At 07.40 a Halifax called up Carnaby to say it could not get its undercarriage locked. It was instructed to land on the centre runway three quarters way along, travelling from east to west. The aircraft touched down at 07.45 with the undercarriage down but one of the wheels failed to lock, resulting in the aircraft swinging round 180° and blocking the centre runway. It had hardly settled when a second Halifax with a burst tyre called Carnaby for assistance. This aircraft was instructed to touch down early on the runway owing to the obstruction at the far end of the runway. It did so but also swung round and completely blocked the other end of the runway.

The second aircraft landed just 12 minutes after the first, but by the time it was touching down, the first aircraft was already on the move, due to the efforts of the crash gang. In five minutes the first aircraft was clear of the runway and in another ten minutes all three runways were clear of obstructions and ready for anymore aircraft that might come in".

158 Squadron – 14th October 1944

Orders were received to carry out Operation Hurricane on the 14th October 1944. Operation Hurricane was a special raid in partnership with the VIIIth United States Bomber Command to bomb the densely populated Ruhr area. Duisburg was to be the main target and to maximise impact, the operation would be divided into two waves. The first wave consisted of 1,013 British aircraft and a staggering 3,574 tons of high explosives and 820 tons of incendiaries would be dropped on the city. The American contingent would then send a further 1,251 heavy bombers backed up by 749 fighters. Later on the same day a further 1,005 aircraft would be dispatched by Bomber Command, again in two forces, two hours apart. Another 4,040 tons of high explosives and 500 tons of incendiaries would then be dropped on Duisburg during the night. The result was catastrophic damage to building and the loss of about eight days of production.

Britain suffered a few aircraft loses on this raid and many aircraft were damaged due to flak. Those on the first wave took the heaviest losses and flak damage. One of those aircraft, a Handley Page Halifax B, Mk III (MZ928 NP-S), piloted by Flight Lieutenant Donald Simpson Checklin DFC, was seriously damaged by anti-aircraft fire over the target and the port inner engine was put out of commission.

© IWM (CE 161).
Flight Lieutenant Donald Simpson Checklin DFC (158 Squadron, Lissett, Yorkshire) inspecting his aircraft after safely landing at Carnaby. (This story has been verified by the Curator of 158 Squadron).

The story of F/Lt Checklin….

F/Lt Checklin and his crew had left their base at RAF Lissett at 06.40 on the 14th October 1944. They had a clear view over the target, apart from smoke rising as bombs rained down on the city. Their route was peppered by flak but they continued on to their target and dropped their bomb load at 09.09 hrs at an altitude of 18, 000ft. Their aircraft was hit by flak as they flew across. Flying Officer F H Greenhalgh, a wireless operator, was injured by shrapnel in his left foot which he quickly bandaged. F/Lt Checklin completed his bombing run then headed for home but the flak damage had caused the propeller and reduction gear to shear off. It then smashed into the fuselage of their aircraft, resulting in a rather large, gaping hole, just where

F/O Greenhalgh was sitting. Luckily, for Greenhalgh he had shifted his position whilst nursing his injured foot, thus saving his legs from being sliced off. F/Lt Checklin valiantly flew his stricken bomber all the way back to England, despite the critical state of his aircraft. He headed for Carnaby and made a safe landing. F/O Greenhalgh was taken immediately to the hospital at the airfield where he received treatment for his wounds resulting in the partial amputation of his 2nd and 3rd toes. Later on, F/Lt Checklin was awarded the Distinguished Flying Cross (DFC) for his bravery in bringing home a seriously crippled bomber. He was mentioned in dispatches posted in the London Gazette (17th July 1944).

F/Lt Checklin's courage was mentioned again in an Air Ministry Bulletin (19245). The citation of which reads:

> *"This officer has completed a large number of operational sorties during which he has attacked many of the most heavily defended targets in Germany. On one occasion, in October 1944, during an attack on Duisburg, his aircraft was hit by anti-aircraft fire while on the bombing run. One engine was damaged and the wireless operator was wounded. Nevertheless, Flight Lieutenant Checklin pressed on and completed the attack. On the return flight part of the damaged engine broke away and smashed a considerable hole in the fuselage but with great skill this officer flew the crippled aircraft safely back to base. Throughout this incident, this Captain of aircraft displayed coolness and courage and inspired his crew by his determination to overcome all obstacles".*

Two months later, on the 29th December 1944, F/Lt Checklin needed the assistance of Carnaby again, and requiring the assistance of FIDO. He was returning from a bombing mission in Germany to annihilate the marshalling yards in Koblenz.

F/Lt Checklin survived the war and, after leaving the RAF, went on to fly for British South American Airways (BSAA). Unfortunately, he was killed in an air crash in a Lancastrian III, G AGWH "Star Dust". He was the 3rd pilot on this aircraft which was lost on the 2nd August 1947 when it came down in the Andes Mountain, South America. The wreckage was only discovered in 2000 by an Argentine Army expedition at the top of the Tupungato glacier, 80 miles east of Santiago, Chile. He is now buried in the British Cemetery in Buenos Aires. He was born in Leeds on the 29th May 1920 and joined up in 1940. He was posted to 158 Squadron on the 20th September 1944 and was posted out on 8th April 1945 having flown 38 ops with this Squadron.

16th November 1944

"My account of Flying through Fire" by ex-Air Gunner, Geoff Towers, B.E.M., 158 Squadron.

Geoff Towers B.E.M

"On our homeward leg from Munster, Germany, the fog got worse and worse; it was just like pea soup. Eventually, we were diverted from our home base at RAF Lissett to RAF Emergency base, Carnaby.

I was sitting in my turret thinking this was the worst we had ever seen, when up comes the navigator on the intercom with a startling remark: "ETA in five minutes". I must admit I was very concerned for I knew there was no way in which we would be clear of the fog in that time. I said to myself " this is it, we are going to have to bale out", hoping it would be over the land and not the bloody North Sea. The Skipper's voice came over the intercom: "Geoff, can you see anything shining from the deck, through the fog?" I replied "You must be joking Skip, I can't even see the end of my gun barrels!"

I was just about to say my prayers when I looked out of the side of my turret and I could see a bright glow in the sky from below the fog. I informed the Skipper over the intercom. We started to descend and then I could see the runway with fire on each side. I did not know much about FIDO at that time, although I had heard of it. The Skipper did a couple of circuits and we landed at 5.30 on the 16th November 1944.

It is certainly a memory that will always stay with me. We got transport to our home base Lissett and to the Mess for bacon and eggs."

Crew of Halifax "K" King, 158 Squadron

This is the second time that Sergeant Towers had landed at Carnaby. The first recorded time was on the night of the 5th/6th December 1944, flying back from the Ruhr when his Halifax III, "K" MZ480 was hit by flak whilst flying at 13,000ft. The pilot, F/O Sharp, was forced to land at Carnaby due to hydraulics failure.

76 Squadron

On the 3rd and 4th March 1945, Bomber Command took to the skies again on another bombing raid. A total of 234 aircraft, 201 Halifaxes of 4 Group, 21 Lancasters and 12 Mosquitoes of 8 Group, headed for the synthetic-oil refinery in Kamen, near Dortmund. The plant was covered by thin cloud with fleeting breaks in between. They sustained a concentrated attack. The oil refinery was severely damaged by accurate bombing and oil production ceased immediately. Twenty aircraft from 76 Squadron, based at Holme-Upon-Spalding Moor, made a very successful bombing raid.

However, upon returning to their base they were attacked by enemy night fighters and one Halifax bomber, NA584, Aircraft "E", piloted by P/O P Oleynik RCAF, was badly damaged and had to be diverted to Carnaby. P/O Oleynik had attacked his primary target at 22.05hrs and the records show that the crew had a successful bombing raid as they reported seeing black smoke rising from the oil tank they had just bombed. Enemy night fighters attacked their aircraft on the return journey, damaging their aircraft and fatally wounding Mid Upper Gunner, F/Sgt William Thomas Maltby. P/O Oleynik made a crash landing at 01.10hrs and finished up among some parked aircraft. Unfortunately, Maltby died of a serious head injury. He was only 19 years old and haled from Kamloops in British Columbia. He was posthumously promoted to Pilot Officer after his death and is buried in Stonefall Cemetery, near Harrogate.

Diversions

Diversions to Carnaby began almost immediately. The first entry in the operations book shows that on the 18th April 1944, a Mosquito from No 13 OTU was diverted to Carnaby because the pilot was lost and had flat batteries. A few days later on the 25th April, two Halifax bombers were diverted from RAF Lissett because of a shortage of fuel. Landings occurred almost daily, with Halifax bombers being the most predominant aircraft to land there. The first largest contingency of diversions occurred on the 8th June 1944 when 29 Halifaxes from 4 Group and two Lancasters from 5 Group landed during the early morning.

Aircrew from 51 Squadron landed at Carnaby on the 3rd September 1944

A few months later, on the 3rd September 1944, 14 Halifaxes from 51 Squadron were diverted due to prevailing weather conditions at their base, eight of these aircraft had been damaged but the rest were purely diversions. One aircraft crash landed at Withern, they were returning home from a very successful bombing raid on the Venlo airfield in Holland. This airfield was of great importance to the Germans as it was one of the major bases protecting the Ruhr area. It was a well-equipped airbase and straddled both sides of the Dutch/German border. In all, 675 aircraft set off that day to bomb six airfields in Southern Holland. All raids were successful but one Halifax was lost.

November the same year, saw a diversion of 20 Lancasters land at Carnaby on all the same day. Difficulties arose with the dispersing of aircraft as there was a lack of hard standing and a waterlogged airfield. Carnaby was not equipped to accommodate large numbers of aircrew and it became an increasing problem.

On the 16th November 1944, 42 Fortresses, 11 Mosquitoes and a mixture of 18 other aircraft were diverted to Carnaby, totalling 71 aircraft in all. The arrival of so many aircraft and crews created an administrative nightmare for Carnaby. Accommodation and messing had to be found for over 600 aircrew, many of whom were Americans. With the co-operation of nearby bases at RAF Lissett, Catfoss, Driffield and Leconfield accommodation was found for them all. RAF Lissett and Catfoss took the brunt of the extra responsibilities for which the Station Commander at Carnaby was particularly grateful. However, their problems were far from over as all aircraft were grounded the next day due to poor weather conditions. Luckily, no further aircraft arrived until the 18th November when another 17 aircraft were diverted to Carnaby. Appalling weather conditions had turned the airfield into a quagmire making it difficult for maintenance and service crews to carry out essential repairs. This delayed aircraft leaving for their operational bases and greatly stretched the resources at Carnaby and other nearby RAF stations. Thankfully, the weather picked up and many of the Fortresses were airborne again later that day.

With so much use, the dispersal loop needed constant attention to keep it roadworthy and a shortage of labour did not improve the situation. Accommodation was an ongoing issue and was frequently commented upon.

A month later, Carnaby saw another influx of diversions when 20 Halifaxes landed within 40 minutes on the eve of the 21st December. The next day 13 Fortresses were diverted from 482 USAAF and then on the 24th December a further 62 aircraft were diverted, followed by 20 more Halifaxes on the 26th. Carnaby was stretched to its limits and an urgent request was put into assist the Station in carrying out its work. The Station Commander asked for one Nissen hut Briefing Room to be used as Aircrew Reception, six additional aircrew coaches, three additional David Brown tractors, one crane for engine changes, three trailers for sanding the runway, two additional Fordson tractors, one Petrol Tanker, two 45 gallon Oil Bowsers, one low loading trailer with winch, one Off Loading Transport, twenty additional F.C.A.s for the operation of the FIDO installation and six more Nissen Huts for accommodation. He completed his order stating that that this Station was never designed to handle 102 aircraft in two days and therefore it was essential that this equipment was provided immediately.

A lot of valuable time was used in ferrying the aircrews to other bases during these large diversion. This coupled with a number of overseas postings, left Carnaby short of staff, especially to operate the FIDO installation. They now only had 19 men to operate 60 control pits, each valve needed to be manned during a full burn to assist aircraft in distress. Ice on the runway was also creating a major problem, it was half an inch deep and it took 80 men to throw salt and sand over it to thaw it out. Carnaby faced more problems during the month of December when on six occasions, it was noted that there were more than 25 aircraft parked on the edge of the runway as the dispersal loop was full. This posed a great risk to incoming aircraft but was a risk they had to take.

In January 1945, there were more diversions, with 21 aircraft arriving on the 14th, 27 arrived the following day, then 35 aircraft the day after that. The last day of January saw a massive influx of 65 Liberators and 6 Halifaxes. By the end of the month, a total of 279 landings were made, 123 being emergency landings and the remaining 156 being diversions, FIDO was used 76 times due to fog and low cloud. Again, RAF Lissett bore the brunt of accommodating and feeding the 700 aircrew. Transporting the crews to RAF Lissett was once again troublesome but by impressing all vehicles on the camp into service all crews were eventually dispersed and cared for. RAF Lissett had to convert an Old Sergeant's Mess into an aircrew reception areas in order to deal with the 700 aircrew that landed at Carnaby. The local Army was drafted into RAF Carnaby to help deal with the shortage of labour which eased the burden somewhat but by no means resolved all their problems.

February continued to see regular diversions and emergencies, the largest being on the 21st February when 12 Halifaxes, 3 Lancasters, 1 Liberator and 1 Stirling were forced to land at Carnaby. The Station suffered a severe setback when the Army attachment was withdrawn, this affected operational and sectional duties. RAF Snaith came to their rescue and sent a temporary flight attachment but this too was short-lived as many of the flights were then discharged to the army, once again leaving Carnaby short of labour.

The month of March saw a break in the weather conditions, this combined with a relaxation of operational duties helped to improve the general cleanliness of the Station. However, conditions in Europe were not as favourable and a surprise landing by the famous Dambusters' Squadron, 617 Squadron, were diverted to Carnaby. A total of 17 Lancasters arrived from this squadron alone, along with six other heavy bombers and one Spitfire with unserviceable hydraulics. On the 25th another large diversion headed to RAF Carnaby with the arrival of 26 Halifaxes. It was assumed that RAF Lissett would once again be asked to accommodate the aircrews!

By now, Britain and her allies were winning the war in Europe and preparations for "V" Day were already being planned. Officers at RAF Carnaby were instructed on their responsibilities and greater emphasis was put upon the general welfare of the Station to prepare for the cessation of hostilities. More diversion occurred in April when 24 Halifaxes were diverted to RAF Carnaby and required the assistance of FIDO for a safe landing. By VE Day, RAF Carnaby had assisted 1,485 aircraft to land safely. Aircraft continued to land on a regular basis at the airfield for several months after and continued to do so until March 1946. The airfield was then decommissioned as an emergency runway.

Chapter 5
617 Squadron and the Grand Slam Bombs

Of all the squadrons in Bomber Command there are none more famous than the magnificent 617 Squadron, more widely known as "The Dambusters". It therefore may come as a big surprise to many that this famous squadron landed at Carnaby on the evening of the 13th March 1945. Actually, they were diverted here due to poor weather conditions having set off on their special mission. It is rumoured that the Squadron used the airfield prior to this for practicing take offs with a special cargo bound for Germany.

At exactly 18.07 hours on the 13th March 1945, the first Lancaster touched down followed by the rest of the squadron. By 18.28 hours all 17 Lancasters had landed safely and without incident at Carnaby Airfield. They were led by Group Captain J Fauquier DSO, DFC, who was a former Canadian bush pilot. Fauquier had taken command of 617 Squadron in December 1944 having previously commanded 405 (Vancouver) Squadron, which was the Canadian PFF (Pathfinder) Squadron. Pathfinders were famous for their precision in marking bomb targets ahead of the main task force.

Bielefeld viaduct.

The intended target for 617 Squadron that evening was to bomb the Bielefeld Railway Viaduct in Germany which connected the Ruhr Valley to Berlin over the River Werre. Previous attempts with Tallboy bombs had failed to make any permanent damage. The viaduct was too well made and the 12,000 lb Tallboy bombs were just not powerful enough to destroy it. The viaduct was a substantial structure standing at a height of 73 feet, 27 feet wide and had 26 arches each with a span of 46 feet. The full length was approximately 1,100 feet. Bielefeld was an industrial town that mass produced war material from hand guns to anti-tank weapons as well as aircraft and tank parts. The Hamm-Wunsdorf section of the Bielefeld viaduct carried the heaviest tonnage of freight in the whole of Germany and more than 300 trains per day carried war material straight to Berlin. It was therefore vital for Britain to destroy the heart of Germany's war production and to stop arms reaching Berlin, the Viaduct therefore had to be taken out. Bielefeld was also an important control point for large numbers of Wermacht troops as they were moved between the various front lines and therefore it was another considerable motive for targeting this town.

However, the viaduct was not an easy target. It was well protected by an air observation post coupled with smoke generators which concealed the viaduct from airborne attacks when operated. A flak gun battery (20mm) was manned by 24 men from above the viaduct and on the viaduct itself was a Vierling Cannon. British Bombers therefore had to be extremely vigilant and well prepared when attacking this target. Previous attempts by the RAF to bomb this viaduct had failed to make any lasting impact on the structure itself. A few bent tracks were really the most damage caused and were quickly repaired. In February 1945, 617 Squadron had dropped several Tallboy bombs on the viaduct but the viaduct held fast. To destroy this target it would require an explosion of such huge magnitude as to shake the very foundations of the viaduct itself. The answer came with the invention of Sir Barnes Wallis's "Grand Slam" bomb, better known as the "Earthquake bomb".

The Grand Slam bomb was the heaviest bomb ever made during WW2. It was designed to be dropped from a great height. It weighed 22,000 lbs, was 26ft long with a diameter of 5ft. The casing was cast from a special chrome molybdenum steel and inside, was filled with 9,975 lbs of Torpex (Torpedo Explosives). Torpex was a powerful combination of RDX, TNT and powdered aluminium. The only problem with this bomb was that it was too heavy for most bombers to carry. The only bomber that was capable of carrying it was the Lancaster but even that had to be modified and strengthened. Carrying such a heavy weight meant that there were sacrifices to be made. Two Lancasters were modified but had to sacrifice two members of their crew, the Wireless Operator and the Mid-Upper Gunner, in order to carry its heavy load; the mid upper turret was also removed.

Two of the Lancasters that landed at Carnaby carried the notorious Grand Slam bombs. Group Captain J Fauquier and Squadron Leader Charles Calder were the pilots of these specially modified Lancasters which bore the new marking of "YZ" rather than "AJ". Their aircrew had been reduced to five instead of the usual seven. The extra weight of these bombs was just too great for even the magnificent Lancaster to cope with and fly with a full complement of aircrew!

On the 13th March, poor weather conditions in Germany resulted in aborting the mission and Group Captain Fauquier made the choice of landing at Carnaby instead of their usual base at Woodhall Spa. The decision to do so was based on the fact that two of the bombers were still heavily laden with the ten-ton bomb load and would need a considerable runway to provide the "lift" that was required to get these bombers airborne once again. Carnaby was perfect. It had one of the longest and widest runways in England and it was also near the coast. The arrival of this special cargo went down in history. Fauquier and Calder were the first pilots to land their aircraft with a ten-ton bomb still on board. In the Station's Operating Records' book from RAF Station Carnaby, their arrival was noted with interest and read:

> *"From 18.07 to 18.28 hours 17 Lancasters of 617 Squadron were recalled owing to weather and diverted to Carnaby, all landing without incident. This Squadron was on a special mission and two of the aircraft carried the new 22,500 lb [sic] bombs, being dropped for the first time on Germany".*

The Squadron presumably were accommodated at RAF Lissett until the next day as Carnaby had limited accommodation. However, no further information has been recorded with regards to this fact..

On the 14th March at 02.15, 617 Squadron took off from Carnaby Airfield on their special mission to bomb the Bielefeld Railway Viaduct in Germany. Two of the Lancasters had the Grand Slam bombs, the rest were fitted with Tallboy bombs. Unfortunately, on take-off Group Captain J Fauquier failed to get off the ground at Carnaby owing to engine trouble. A connecting rod had broken and the bomb-sight was unserviceable due to an oil leak, leaving the Squadron not only one aircraft short but also one Grand Slam bomb short as well. Fauquier's aircraft was one of the modified Lancasters fitted with the Grand Slam bombs. Calder noticed that Fauquier was having trouble with his Lancaster; however, he either ignored the signal from Fauquier or failed to understand the order in which he was being told to switch aircraft and instead took-off leaving a frustrated and angry Fauquier running down the runway trying in vain to stop him.

Squadron Leader Jock Calder.

The impact of this shortfall was recorded in the daily operations log book at Carnaby:

"Germany had short weight on this delivery. An opportunity of remedying this deficiency however will no doubt be presented in the very near future"

The Squadron's Operation's Record Book shows that only 15 Lancasters flew on to Bielefeld. With Fauquier unable to get off the ground, the raid was then led by Squadron Leader Charles "Jock" Calder.

The Squadron was escorted to Bielefeld by eight squadrons of Mustangs and four Mosquitos from 8 PFF Group. They reached the viaduct later that afternoon. At precisely 16.28 hours, Calder dropped his Grand Slam bomb from a height of 11,965 ft. It landed approximately 30 yards away from the target, creating a crater of 100 feet deep. The bomb-aimer, C B Crafer, reported afterwards in his log book *"Direct hit with 23,000 [sic] bomb (first to be dropped)"*. The rest of the Squadron then pummelled the viaduct with a torrent of Tallboy bombs. The impact from the Grand Slam bomb undermined the viaduct itself and with the aid of the Tallboy bombs the job was completed when a massive section of five arches finally collapsed, rendering the viaduct unserviceable for the rest of the war. The victorious Squadron then headed for home and all arrived safely back at their bases by 8pm that night and, no doubt, a well-earned drink! Crafer recorded in his Observer's and Air Gunner's Flying Log Book that it took a mere 4 hours and 50 minutes flying time to complete his mission to bomb the Bielefeld viaduct and land safely at his base.

The Germans however, realised that the viaduct was a strategic target and therefore had made provisions just in case it was targeted and bombed out of action. The Germans had ingeniously built a "viaduct by-pass" but the new by-pass had to be built on steep slopes which severely restricted the speed of the trains. The Germans also had to deploy extra locomotives to help push exceptionally heavy goods' trains up the steepest of hills. The line was nicknamed "Gummibahn" (Rubber Railway) because the line was so shaky and was no match for the defunct viaduct. It may not have halted the production and logistics of war material getting to Berlin but it did slow it down enough to have some impact on the war effort and was a great success for the men of 617 Squadron. The viaduct was so badly damaged it remained closed for the rest of the war. It has since been repaired and is still in use today.

Chapter 6
Friends and Allies

The British Government relied on help from its Commonwealth countries to come to her aid as hostilities broke out in Europe. Britain was desperately short of trained aircrew, and in particular, pilots and navigators. Aircraft production was rapidly out-stripping the numbers of trained aircrew available to fly them. Training aircrew in Britain posed several obstacles; there was not enough space for training due to a shortage of airfields; and the current airfields were susceptible to attack from the German Luftwaffe.

A plan was therefore devised by the British Government and put to its dominions to jointly train and supply aircrew to serve with the RAF. After weeks of negotiations an agreement was finally signed in Ottawa, Canada on the 17th December 1939. Canada, Australia, and New Zealand all signed the agreement. The plan was known as the British Commonwealth Air Training Plan (BCATP). In Australia, the plan was known as the Empire Air Training Scheme (EATS). Part of the Agreement, Article XV, proposed that each country had its own distinct national squadrons. Canada had immediately negotiated a deal for distinct Royal Canadian Air Force (RCAF) squadrons to be formed, and ultimately created its own group as well - 6 (RCAF) Group. Australia had 17 dedicated squadrons (numbers 450-467), however the majority of their airmen served in RAF squadrons. New Zealand had seven dedicated squadrons which were mainly fighter squadrons.

By the end of the war 151 training schools were established across Canada. Rhodesia was also used to train aircrew through the Rhodesia Air Training Group (RATG). These training schools produced 131,553 aircrew for the RAF and the Commonwealth Countries. This included aircrew from other countries such as Poland, Norway, Belgium and Holland, and Czechoslovakia.

It was not only the Commonwealth countries that fought alongside the RAF. After the fall of France, many French squadrons found themselves both homeless and country-less. Some of these squadrons, which were fighting abroad in North Africa, formed the Free French Air Force (FFAF) who then volunteered to serve alongside the RAF. They were posted to

England and many were based at RAF Driffield, Leconfield and Elvington. Elvington was an all French base.

Without their help and support Britain would surely have fallen under the strain. All gave some and some gave all. It is therefore important that we pay respect to all the nations that fought alongside the RAF, regardless of their nationality. Without the devotion to do their duty, their commitment and most of all for their bravery in volunteering to defend a country that most had never been to before.

Digging deep into the archives at Kew, it is fitting that some of their stories are told. They deserve to be remembered and honoured for the sacrifices they made for our freedom. Here are just a few of their stories….

The Australians

460 RAAF Squadron

3rd August 1944

Over 1,100 aircraft were detailed to attack flying bomb storage sites in France. Australian squadron No 460 were instructed to bomb the flying-bomb site at Trossy St Maxim. More than 600 Lancasters were involved that night. Pilot Officer N J Noxley, flying his Lancaster ND 822, was on course to bomb this site when his aircraft flew into heavy flak. His aircraft was badly holed on the leading edge of his starboard wing and fluid started to pour out. Unfortunately, he mistook the leak to be petrol and went onto to bomb the site at 14.15pm at a height of 13,000 feet.

The fuel leak was in fact hydraulic fluid, which meant that the bomb doors would not open. The bomb-aimer had incorrectly assumed that it was an electrical supply fault. When the bomb doors failed to open they had no option but to return to base. With the main hydraulic system unserviceable, Noxley was forced to make an emergency landing at Carnaby with a full bomb load still on board! A very dangerous thing to do. Luckily, he and his crew made a safe landing.

14th January 1945

On the 14th January 1945, 573 Lancasters and 14 Mosquitoes carried out attacks on synthetic oil plants at Leuna. Severe damage was caused to the plant but resulted in the loss of 10 Lancaster bombers. Two Lancasters from No 460 Squadron were forced to land at Carnaby having had to abort their missions. One Lancaster, flown by Australian Pilot Officer Maton (Lancaster PB 352), had developed a petrol leak and was diverted to Carnaby, the second, piloted by Flying Officer Marshall, had to abort his mission due to one of his crew becoming sick during the raid. That night, three aircrew were admitted to the sick quarters at Carnaby. One was a navigator who collapsed shortly after setting course, a rear-gunner was air sick and had catarrh and the third patient was an observer who had fallen ill on the way out suffering with coryza (head cold). All three were deemed fit to fly back to their units the following day.

That night was a busy night for Carnaby with two Fortresses from 100 Group making an emergency landing, followed by a Lancaster short of fuel, then a Wellington with instruments u/s, six Halifaxes, one Martinet and finally 10 Lancasters.

462 RAAF Squadron

27th August 1944

Destination Homberg – Rheinpreussen synthetic-oil refinery at Meerbeck. Bomber squadrons were detailed to attack the synthetic-oil refineries in Homberg on the 27th August 1944. This was the first major daylight raid since August 1941 and to ensure their safety nine Spitfire squadrons escorted the bombers to Germany. Intense flak was encountered over the target area, damaging several aircraft. Ten Lancasters from No 462 Squadron were dispatched that day. One returned safely on three engines to its base at Driffield, the second piloted by Australian Flying Officer Cuttriss (Halifax III LV 955), had to abort his mission shortly after take-off. The port outer CSU became u/s, Cuttriss tried to feather the airscrew, unfortunately this did not work resulting in both the airscrew and reduction gear falling off. They jettisoned their bombs to lighten the load. With one propeller missing they headed for Carnaby and an emergency landing. However, the mid-upper gunner, Australian Sgt Dyer, made the decision to bail out over Flamborough Head. The remainder of the crew made a safe landing at Carnaby despite having one propeller missing. All the crew, including Dyer who had returned back safely from his adventures over Flamborough Head, were in Ops again on the 31st August 1944.

F/O AG Cuttriss 410634   *Sgt WE Dyer 427638*

(printed by kind permissions granted by John Dann)

463 RAAF Squadron

8/9th February 1945 (Air 27/1922)

A Lancaster (ED611 JO.U) of 463 RAAF (Royal Australian Air Force) was on a bombing raid to Politz when it was attacked by a night fighter (JU88), resulting in their No 1 port tank catching fire and the hydraulics being severely damaged and the MUG intercom tubes severed. They still had 5 minutes to go before bombing time. They managed to shake off the fighters, pressing on to the bomb target. They bombed their target and then immediately proceeded to feather the port inner engine but the fire intensified and two minutes after bombing they were attacked by another fighter. The Lancaster went into a corkscrew to try and put out the blaze. It was dimmed but not extinguished. The pilot, F/O M S Wickes ordered the crew to stand by ready to abandon the aircraft. In a last attempt to put out the flames he went into a steep dive and was successful and the flames went out. They were now flying on 3 engines. Both of the Gunners' intercoms by this time were u/s but despite this the rear-gunner was able to shoot down a JU88. Wickes commended him on his "excellent performance" under trying circumstances. The rear-gunner also gave a running commentary to the pilot of how to avoid other night fighters in the sky. The pilot highly commended the co-operation of his team and his navigator was able to direct them over Denmark to make a safe landing at Carnaby. Sgt Botting, the Engineer, praised his pilot F/O Wickes over his

48

"magnificent performance in keeping the crew calm and calculated and making a perfect landing when all the time he knew the a/c was hardly air worthy".

6th October 1944

On the 6th October 1944 a daylight operation of 320 aircraft were dispatched to attack the synthetic-oil plants at Sterkrade. The weather conditions were clear and the bombing was considered to be accurate. However, heavy flak was encountered with the loss five aircraft and a large percentage of aircraft were damaged. Five Halifaxes landed at Carnaby that day including two Australian pilots from No 462 Squadron. Pilot Officer FH James (Halifax III NR119) was the first to land due to having hydraulic trouble and flak damage, following closely behind was W/O DM Taylor (Halifax III NP 989), who was forced to make an emergency landing when the ASI unit became unserviceable.

The following month two more Australian pilots required the assistance of Carnaby.

4th November 1944

Fifteen aircraft from No 462 Squadron were detailed for a night attack on the town of Bochum in the Ruhr area of Germany. This was the heart of industrial Germany and was the source of an important steel plant – Bochumer Verein. A force of 749 aircraft (384 Halifaxes, 336 Lancasters and 29 Mosquitoes) attacked the city, causing devastation to more than 4,000 buildings. The industrial area was also severely damaged. German night fighters were very active that night causing a lot of casualties.

The Free French Squadron No 346 lost 5 out of 16 Halifaxes during that raid. Fortunately, No 462 Squadron fared better. Two of their aircraft had to abort the mission due to technical difficulties. The oxygen line in the Mid Upper Turret of Halifax MZ431, flown by F/Lt PH Finley broke, resulting in an emergency landing at Carnaby. The second aircraft to land at Carnaby from No 462 Squadron was Halifax III NA621, piloted by Pilot Officer Byrom, did manage to bomb his target, however his aircraft was damaged by flak resulting in a loss of hydraulics.

It was a busy night for Carnaby with 15 Halifax bombers and one Lancaster bomber making emergency landings due to heavy flak damage. The Lancaster was the only aircraft that could be airborne again that day.

467 (RAAF) Squadron

28/29th October 1944 (AIR 27/1931)

A large task force of 237 Lancasters set off to Bergen in Norway to attack U-boat pens but due to dense cloud the mission was aborted. Only 47 Lancasters were able to drop their load due to poor visibility. The Master Bomber then called off the raid. On returning to England a Lancaster III (LM746) of No 467 (RAAF) Squadron collided with another Lancaster I from the same squadron at Bridderby at 23.45, still fully laden with 12 x 1000 lb bombs on board. The Lancaster III had to jettison its bombs 30 miles off the coast of Mablethorpe at 8000 ft. Then four of its crew bailed out, leaving the pilot, navigator and Flight Engineer on board. They made a safe landing at Carnaby even though the port wing had sustained severe damage during the collision. The other aircraft (Lancaster I) although damaged was able to make it safely to its base at RAF Waddington. The crew all taking up crash positions on landing, touching down on one wheel and the aircraft listing to starboard. It had taken the pilot two attempts to land due to the poor visibility. Both crews were mainly Australians.

This also proved to be another busy night for Carnaby. During the early hours of the 28th a Halifax II with no flaps made an emergency landing, then two Halifax III's with no brakes came in, followed by a Lancaster with hydraulics u/s then another with flaps u/s. Later that evening a Lancaster III limped in with port inner engine u/s and hydraulics u/s, followed by three Halifaxes which had been diverted from their base, then another Halifax made a 3 engine landing, then Lancaster LM 746 landed following its collision having made a "Darky" call, then to finish off the day 19 Halifaxes were diverted to Carnaby as well. All in all a busy night for the Carnaby Crew who deserve to be mentioned for all their hard work and in efficiency at clearing the runways.

The Free French Air Force (FFAF)

In 1944 two new squadrons joined the RAF. These squadrons were all French including their Commanding Officer but the adjutant was English. Many of these airmen had been serving in North Africa with the French Air Force but after the invasion of France by Germany they were unable to return home. They then reformed as the Free French Air Force (FFAF) under the control of the RAF and were stationed at RAF Elvington until the end of the war. Over 2000 French airmen served at this air base, working alongside the RAF and Commonwealth aircrews.

In May 1944, the first FFAF squadron, No 346 Squadron (Guyenne), relocated to England and was based at Elvington. It had reformed from the French Groupe 2/23 "Guyenne". A month later the second Squadron arrived in Elvington, formerly known as Groupe 1/25 "Tunisie", and was renamed No. 347 Squadron (Tunisie). These newly formed squadrons came under the control of 4 Group, flying the heavy Halifax bombers. Within ten months these squadrons had flown over 2000 missions, had lost 30 aircraft and over 200 French airmen.

The first operational mission for No 346 Squadron was on the night of the 1st June 1944 when 11 Halifaxes bombed a radar station at Ferme d'Urville. Their last mission was on the 25th April 1945 when they attacked the gun batteries on the island of Wangerooge. In total, No 346 Squadron carried out 1,479 operational sorties from British soil.

The first mission for No 347 Squadron took place on the 27th June 1944. They headed to Mont Candon to bomb a V-weapon site. Twelve Halifaxes took to the skies that night but only eleven completed their mission; the last aircraft had to abort. Their last mission was on also the 25th April 1945 when they joined forces with No 346 Squadron to attack the gun batteries at Wangerooge. At the end of the war they had completed 1,355 sorties.

As Elvington airbase was only 40 miles south of Flamborough Head, Carnaby was often used by both of these Squadrons. Diversions were commonplace due to poor weather conditions at their own base, but as the war progressed these Squadrons relied on the assistance of RAF Carnaby as they struggled to keep their aircraft airborne. These are just a few of their stories....

346 Squadron

12th June 1944

Fourteen aircraft from 346 Squadron were detailed to attack communications, mostly railways in France at Amiens Longueau. Bombing was concentrated and considered to be accurate. Slight heavy flak was encountered in the target area but enemy fighters were very active especially on the return journey over France. Many aircraft were damaged during this raid. One such bomber, a Halifax V (LK 955) piloted by Adj Croblan of No 346 Squadron, was attacked by a single engined enemy fighter. Croblan's aircraft was extensively damaged by flak. He returned fire onto the fighter in defence but failed to shoot it down. He managed to fly his crippled plane safely back to England, heading for the nearest runway at Carnaby. Despite extensive damage miraculously no airmen were injured, however the aircraft was written off and probably scrapped at Carnaby. Although the raid had been successful 23 aircraft were lost that night, 17 of these were Halifaxes and the rest were Lancasters. A heavy loss by any standards.

3rd September 1944

On the 3rd September 1944, the RAF switched their interest into bombing six airfields in Southern Holland which were being used as night fighter bases by the mighty German Luftwaffe. From these bases night-fighters were able to attack British bombers as they flew over Holland on their way to Germany. Fourteen aircraft from No 346 Squadron were detailed to attack Venlo airfield. Venlo airfield was of the largest and most well protected airbases outside of Germany. Over 400 Allied bombers had been shot down from this airbase alone. It was therefore imperative that this airbase was taken out of action. Thirteen aircraft from 346 Squadron successfully attacked this airfield, the fourteenth aircraft suffered engine trouble before reaching the Dutch coast and dropped behind. However, the pilot courageously carried on, eventually joining another stream to bomb Volkel instead. The attack started at 17.31 hrs at a height of 17,000 feet and was completed four and half minutes later. The Squadron encountered heavy flak during the bombing raid and four aircraft were damaged. One of the damaged bombers, a Halifax III (LW 438), piloted by Lt Beraud was forced to land at Carnaby due to minor damage to his aircraft. Another 13 Halifaxes also landed at Carnaby that night. It had been a big raid with 675 aircraft taking part, (348 Lancasters, 315 Halifaxes, and 12 Mosquitoes). Sadly, one Halifax bomber was lost from the Venlo air raid. A few months later on the 22nd January 1945 Halifax LW 438 swung on take-off and was written off.

22nd/23rd January 1945

On the night of 22nd January 1945, thirteen Halifax bombers from No 346 Squadron were detailed to attack Gelsenkirchen. They were part of a much large contingent of 152 bombers, mainly Halifaxes. The attack began at 22.30 hours from a height of 14,500 to 20,100 feet and lasted eight minutes. Most of the bombers dropped their bomb load right on target, causing damage to residential and industrial areas. The raid was deemed successful, however, aircrew were subjected to a barrage of moderate to intense flak during the attack. One aircraft, Halifax III MZ488 piloted by CMT R Barrat (FFAF) was severely hit by flak. Barrat had dropped his bomb load on the intended target, which was illuminated by red target indicators, from a height of 18,000 feet. Unfortunately, his aircraft sustained severe damage to the starboard engine and port outer CSU. Despite this Barrat managed to keep his crippled bomber airborne long enough to reach the safety of the shores of England. Upon reaching the east coast, Barrat took the decision to land at the nearest runway and set a course for Carnaby. The weather conditions were poor and visibility at Carnaby was down to 3,000 yards due to fog. Unable to see the runway Carnaby gave the order for FIDO to be lit. Thankfully, Barrat made a skilful landing at Carnaby at 01.20 hrs on the morning of the 23rd January 1944. The raid had been successful and no aircraft were lost during this raid. Barrat was awarded the DFC medal on the 9th June 1945.

347 (Tunisie) Squadron

11th September 1944

On the evening of the 11th September 1944, ten aircraft from No 347 Squadron were detailed to attack a synthetic oil plant in the Ruhr area. A contingent of 379 aircraft took part in the raid which included 205 Halifaxes, 154 Lancasters and 20 Mosquitoes. They were escorted by 26 fighter squadrons, (20 Squadrons of Spitfires, 3 Squadrons of Mustangs and 3 Squadrons of Tempests). Thankfully they did not encounter any German fighters but had to endure very heavy flak throughout their raid.

Unfortunately their target, the Nordstern plant, was partially obscured by a smoke-screen. This was purposely created by large generators in order to protect the site from accurate bombing. To make their task even harder, intense and accurate flak began 20 miles before they even reached their target and continued to blight them during the attack and upon their return. Six aircraft from No 347 Squadron were damaged during this raid included the one flown by Lt Deleuze who was forced to land his aircraft (Halifax III LL 557) at Carnaby. He had been on course to bomb the target at 20,000 feet, and at precisely 18.32 hours had dropped his bomb load. Unfortunately, he was unable to observe the results. Seven aircraft were lost during this raid, including one from No 347 Squadron, piloted by Lt Berthet.

Four months later, on the 6th January 1945, Deleuze and his crew were shot down on a raid to Hanover in the same aircraft (LL 557). Two crew were killed, 1 evaded capture and 4 were captured and became Prisoners of War (PoW).

<u>26th December 1944</u>

Three aircraft from No 347 Squadron, piloted by A/C J Aulen, Lt M Candelier and Capt R Bonnett, were detailed to attack German troop positions near St Vith (Battle of the Bulge) during the Ardennes battle. They attacked their target visually and on target indicators at precisely 15.29. The attack took just two minutes from a height of 13,500 to 14,000 feet. Aircraft from all bomber groups had joined together in one attack, with a combination of Lancasters, Halifaxes and Mosquitoes. In total 294 aircraft joined forces in this attack. The attack was deemed very successful despite the loss of two Halifax bombers. On the journey home the weather closed in over Elvington resulting in poor visibility. They took the decision to divert to Carnaby and landed with the assistance of FIDO.

Aulen's crew were shot down on 8th February 1945 on operation to Goch; six were killed, one survived and landed in allied territory. Candelier was awarded the DFC on the 24th July 1945 and Bonnet was awarded the DFC on the 21st August 1944.

On the night of the 17th February 1945, twelve aircraft from No 347 (Tunisie) Squadron, took off from Elvington airfield once again. Their target for the night was to bomb a strategic depot in Wesel, which lay in the heart of the Ruhr Vallley. Unfortunately, the target area was covered in cloud and only eight aircraft out of 298 were able to bomb the target. The Master Bomber decided to abandon the mission and called off the attack. No aircraft were lost during this raid but flak had seriously damaged three Halifaxes which crashed in England. One of those being from No 347 Squadron.

Pilot A/C H Vidal flew his crippled Halifax bomber, LL573 L8-B back to England , which was seriously damaged by flak and its outer port engine was on fire. Unable to return to Elvington, the pilot diverted to Carnaby where it crash landed on the emergency runway and was written off.

The Canadians

Canada entered the war on the 10th September 1939 and in a few short weeks troops were already on their way to the UK to join the British Expeditionary Force (BEF). The Canadian Air Force formed the No. 6 (Royal Canadian Air Force) Bomber Group and operated from Yorkshire. Their badge reflects its origins with a maple leaf superimposed on a York rose. No. 6 (RCAF) Group eventually grew to form 14 heavy bomber squadrons and was completely manned by Canadian officers and men.

No. 405 Squadron was formed at Driffield (which is the parent base of RAF Carnaby) on the 23rd April 1941, initially flying Wellington bombers until 1942. They then converted to Halifax bombers. For a short period of time they were loaned to Coastal Command during convoy movements in the Bay of Biscay. They then returned to Bomber Command in March 1943 under the control of No. 6 (RCAF) Group. After a few weeks they were then selected for No. 9 (Pathfinder) Group until the end of the war and were equipped with Lancasters.

By the end of the war No. 6 Group had flown a total of 40,822 sorties, 814 aircraft were lost and 8,000 medals for bravery were awarded to the aircrew of No.6 Group.

415 Squadron (RCAF)

<u>6th December 1944</u>

Fifteen aircraft from 415 Squadron, based at East Moor, Sutton on Forest, Yorkshire, were detailed to attack the railway yards and factories in Osnabrück. They were part of a much larger assault of 453 aircraft. Flight Lieutenant J R Northrup and his crew were flying in Halifax MZ947 "K". They had a full bomb load of 500 lbs bombs on board and were flying at 18,000ft. Cloud obscured the target, and they were unable to find the Pathfinders target indicators, however they still dropped their bomb load at 19.49 hrs in the hope of hitting their target.

Despite the heavy assault, the raid was only partially successful. The railway yards were slightly damaged and 4 factories, including the Teuto-Metallwerke munitions factory were hit. Many houses were also bombed.

All fifteen aircraft from No 415 Squadron landed safely, however, F/L Northrup was forced to land at Carnaby that night due to lack of brake pressure. He made a safe landing at 22.49 hrs. Seven other Halifaxes and one Lancaster also arrived that night at Carnaby. All aircraft had lost brake pressure presumably due to flak damage over the target area. Sadly, seven Halifaxes and one Lancaster were lost that night.

419 Squadron (RCAF)

<u>20th September 1944</u>

This was a daylight attack on enemy troop concentrations in Calais. A large assault of 646 aircraft took part in this raid, including pilot WO2 LH McDonald of No 419 Squadron, flying Lancaster X (KB 797 "K"). Weather conditions at his base of Middleton-St-George were deemed "not favourable", however the weather over Calais was thought to be fair. The assault schedule was changed from 13.30 hours to 15.30 hours as it was thought the earlier time would have meant a "rush job" and as such was subsequently postponed for 2 hours.

McDonald and his crew left their base at 16.08 hours having been briefed to use new bombing tactics. Many aircraft on this raid were ordered to fly at a height of only 10,000 feet, some were ordered by the Master of Ceremonies to bomb even lower at 6,000 feet. The new tactics used by No 419 Squadron were deemed to be "not particularly satisfactory". However, the overall success of the raid was accurate and well concentrated.

All aircraft were diverted to other bases, presumably due to weather conditions. McDonald was diverted to Carnaby. With visibility down to 1,800 yards due to low cloud and mist, FIDO was lit to aid a safe landing.

420 Squadron (RCAF)

16/17th August 1944

The target for the night was the dock and ship building area of Kiel. P/O Kidd and his crew left their base of Tholthorpe, Yorkshire at 21.22 with a full bomb load. They attacked Kiel at 00.13 ½ hours from a height of 19,000 feet, dropping their bombs on the red and green target indicators dropped by the Pathfinders. They encountered moderate flak over the target. Upon returning to base an aircraft cut across their bow and pilot's canopy, colliding at 01.41, bending both port props. Their starboard tailpipe had also been holed. The pilot, P/O Kidd sustained two fractures of his right arm and facial injuries; the sight of one eye being obstructed during the collision. Despite these injuries P/O Kidd successfully landed his Halifax III (LL589 "N") at Carnaby without injury to his crew. He was later that month posted to 62 Base on sick leave.

429 Squadron

14th October 1944

On the 14th October 1944 a special operation known as Operation Hurricane was ordered by Bomber Command. A command force of both British and USAAF bombers flew just after first light to bomb Duisburg. A total of 1,013 British bombers were dispatched, along with an escort of fighters, carrying 3,574 tons of high explosives and 820 tons of incendiaries. The USAAF send in 1,251 heavy bombers with 749 escort fighters. Later that day a further 1,005 aircraft (498 Lancasters, 468 Halifaxes and 39 Mosquitoes) were sent in two forces, two hours apart, to continue the bombardment of Duisburg. Over 9,000 tons of bombs fell on Duisburg in less than 48 hours, causing severe damage.

RCAF No 429 Squadron were just one of the Squadrons detailed to attack Duisburg that day. P/O Drewery and his crew, flying in a Halifax III ("O" MZ288), attacked one of the alternative targets in Duisburg at 08.48 hrs at a height of 19,000 feet at a speed of 150 mph. Visibility was fair. They bombed the industrial area just west of the Rhine River near the Hoonberg dock area. Moderate flak was encountered and after successfully bombing the area they turned for home. Their hydraulics had been hit by flak and were unserviceable. They were diverted from their base and landed at Carnaby.

424 Squadron

<u>14th October 1944</u>

They were not the only bomber squadron that day to need the assistance of Carnaby. F/O Chance, flying "J" LW 131, on the same bombing run as P/O Drewery also hit flak over the target on the west of the Rhine River, dropping their bombs on the factories in the built up area of Duisburg. F/O Chance's aircraft was hit by flak causing damage to their braking system. With no brake pressure they were diverted to Carnaby for an emergency landing, arriving safely.

New Zealand

In April 1939, Britain and New Zealand held talks in Wellington. It was agreed by both governments that in the event of a war in Europe that the Royal New Zealand Air Force (RNZAF) would provide trained aircrew to the RAF under the British Commonwealth Air Training Plan (BCATP). New flying training schools were soon established at Taieri, Harewood, New Plymouth and Whenuapai to train 700 pilots per year. Observers and air gunners were trained in schools at Ohakea and were to train 730 observers and air gunners per year.

The first New Zealand squadron was No 75 (NZ) Squadron which formed part of the RAF. New Zealand offered 30 Wellington bombers to the UK, along with a full complement of New Zealand air and ground crews. They moved on to fly Stirlings and then changed to Lancasters from 1944 onwards. By the end of the war, New Zealand had trained and supplied 7,002 aircrew. Many of these served in the seven "New Zealand" RAF Squadrons (Nos 485-490), the rest served alongside their British counterparts in RAF Squadrons. Most of these squadrons were fighter squadrons, barring No 487 which was a bomber squadron.

Three New Zealanders won the VC during the war.

100 Squadron

This Squadron was a mixture of aircrew drawn from the four corners of the world, including New Zealand, Australia, South Africa, USA, Poland, Argentina and Canada. It started operations with Bomber Command in 1943, mine laying against U-Boats in St Nazaire.

14th October 1944

On the morning of the 14th October 1944, No 100 Squadron were detailed to attack Duisburg, Germany, as part of Operation Hurricane. They targeted the built up area NE of the steelworks. New Zealand pilot, F/O RJ McVerry, flying in a Lancaster Mk III ("J" ND 326) encountered heavy flak over the target area, sustaining severe damage to his aircraft. The fuselage and tail were badly holed and his hydraulics failed. He was diverted to Carnaby to make an emergency landing.

153 Squadron

30th October 1944

No 153 Squadron was detailed to attack Cologne, 905 aircraft took part in the assault. Seventeen aircraft from No 153 Squadron took off at dusk. Cloud obscured most of their trip but the high medium cloud (up to 24,000 feet) cleared a few miles short of the target. They all bombed on the sky markers before they disappeared into more cloud. Intense heavy flak in barrage form was encountered but fighter activity was only slight. The damage estimated by Bomber Command was thought to be "scattered and light", however the reality was that Cologne sustained heavy bombing, mainly to civilian housing, Cologne University and a 1,000 year old church. The army garrison headquarters took a battering and some railways and public utilities were also hit.

All seventeen aircraft returned safely but aircraft "Q" (Lancaster PB 343) flown by New Zealand pilot F/O RH Williams struck a tree while attempting to land at his base, RAF Scampton, in Lincolnshire. Due to undercarriage damage and one engine out of action he was diverted to Carnaby whereby he made a good landing without further damage to either the aircraft or his crew. It is remarkable that despite damage to his aircraft, and the shock of hitting a tree, that F/O Williams was still able to fly his aircraft several miles away to a small airfield in Yorkshire, when all he really wanted to do was to just land as quickly as possible. His flying skills and bravery are to be greatly admired; to carry on in the face of adversity shows a strength of character that was typical of that era but is rarely found in society today.

158 Squadron

<u>11th April 1945</u>

Over 130 aircraft were detailed to attack the railway yards in Nuremberg. Twenty-five Halifaxes from No 158 Squadron took off from their base at Lissett just at 11.00 hrs. The attack was hailed a success with great accuracy. Heavy flak was encountered damaging six aircraft from No 158 Squadron. One aircraft, piloted by W/O WJ Walsh (NZ), was hit by flak at 15,000 feet whilst bombing the target. His aircraft sustained enough damage for him to be diverted to Carnaby for an emergency landing. Despite the heavy flak, no aircraft were lost during that raid but six aircraft (1 Lancaster and 5 Halifaxes) required the assistance of Carnaby that day, owing to flak damage. All landed safely.

These are of course only a few of the many stories that remain untold. It is, without doubt, that we owe our Commonwealth Countries a debt that can never really be paid. We can however, continue to honour those brave, young airmen and remember what they gave up for us.

Chapter 7
Over paid, over sexed and over here!

It may appear that America did little to help Britain in the first two years of the war. However, their President, Franklin D Roosevelt did aid Britain in a number of ways, but could not provide the much needed manpower and equipment that was so vital to Britain.

The United States of America were keen to avoid embroiling themselves in yet another war and had passed a series of laws in the 1930's to prevent such events happening again. These Acts were known as the Neutrality Acts and prohibited the export of "arms, ammunition and implements of war" from the United States to other nations. Subsequent changes to these Acts further prohibited loans from being provided to "belligerent nations". With the introduction of The Neutrality Act of 1937 even citizens were forbidden from travelling on "belligerent ships" and included the prevention of American merchant ships from carrying any arms to belligerents. This was extended further still to include civil wars. As these Acts had been passed, it limited the help that Roosevelt was able to provide.

Roosevelt had originally opposed this legislation but had to concede due to pressure from Congress and the American public. However, Roosevelt had managed to have one concession to this Act, in that belligerent countries were allowed to acquire any goods other than arms from the United States, (at the discretion of its President). These goods had to be paid for immediately and would not be permitted to be transported on American ships. This system became known as the "cash-and-carry" provision. Raw materials, such as oil, were not considered to be "implements of war" and so therefore could be purchased.

This "cash and carry" clause had been cleverly engineered by Roosevelt to deliberately help countries like Great Britain and France in the event of a war in Europe. These countries, as Roosevelt well knew, were the only countries with enough hard cash and ships to take advantage of this provision. However, this provision was due to expire in just two years' time.

In March 1939, Germany invaded Czechoslovakia causing further concern. Roosevelt tried and failed to renew and expand the "cash and carry" provision to include the sale of arms. Unperturbed, Roosevelt persisted, debating fiercely with Congress until they relented and a final Neutrality Act was passed. This Act lifted the embargo on the sale of arms but remained under the system of the "cash-and-carry" provision.

As the war raged on in Europe, the US Army's Chief of Staff expected Britain to surrender after the fall the of France. However, British tenacity and determination held fast albeit tenuously. Roosevelt, torn between helping Britain and keeping the American public and Congress happy, developed an initiative to help Britain fight the war but to keep America out of it. This new deal was known as "Destroyers for Bases". Britain would receive 50 obsolete US destroyers and, in return, the US would be granted a 99 year lease on air and naval bases in Newfoundland and the Caribbean. Roosevelt persuaded Congress that this deal would ensure of America's continued security as well as keeping the war in Europe at arm's length.

Three months after this agreement, Churchill warned Roosevelt that Britain could no longer afford to pay for goods under the "cash and carry" provision. Roosevelt, once again, came to Britain's aid by proposing a new initiative called "Lend-Lease". Britain would be supplied with the goods needed to fight the war immediately but payment could be deferred to a later date. To ease the burden further payment was not to be in dollars or sterling, instead it would be a joint venture in which the US and Britain would create a liberalised, stable economy in a post-war world. Roosevelt's main objective was to help defeat the Nazis without entering the war, thus again securing peace for America.

The United States of America may well have stayed out of the war were it not for the bombing of Pearl Harbour by the Japanese Pacific Fleet in December 1941. This catastrophic event immediately brought the US into the war. Americans were shocked by this attack which left over 2,400 dead and 21 ships destroyed. Outraged by this attack, the US abandoned its Isolation Policy and immediately declared war on Japan, bringing them promptly into the Second World War. By the 26th January 1942 the first American GI's arrived on British soil.

The British were very relieved when US Troops began arriving in the UK, bringing much needed manpower and arms in the fight to defeat the Nazis. However, the American GI's proved to be too popular with the womenfolk, much to the chagrin of the British men. The GI's were well paid and were more than willing to splash the cash, presenting the British women with much coveted goods such as nylons, chocolates and cigarettes, which had been in short supply since the war started. The British men could not compete. They were poorly paid in comparison to their American counterparts, under-nourished and war weary. Disgruntled they coined the phrase that the American GI's were "Overpaid, over sexed and over here!" In response, the GI's good humouredly retaliated by saying that the British men were "under paid, under sexed and …under Eisenhower!" Touché!

America brought much needed support to Britain, and plenty of it! Support for the RAF came in the form of the mighty US Eighth Air Force, which had over 25 Bomb Groups, equipped with B17 and B24 bombers. The B17 was a large heavy bomber, which was commonly referred to as the Flying Fortress. From January 1943, they flew a staggering 300,000 sorties over Europe. Each bomber had a crew of 10 men and 13 machine guns. It was the most heavily armed bomber in the USAAF. Unlike the RAF, the USAAF took to daylight raids, but they too took heavy losses and had to curtail these raids until the Mustang fighter was introduced. The Mustang was equipped with long-range fuel tanks and could therefore protect the bombers whilst on bombing missions to Europe. The B24 or Liberator was of similar size to the B17 but was much more advanced and had a longer range. It could reach as far the Romanian oil fields from North Africa and was able to attack U-boats in the Atlantic.

These aircraft were also used by the RAF and likewise, the USAAF also flew British built aircraft. Carnaby certainly saw a great deal of American activity over its short existence as an emergency runway. Large numbers of Liberators, Flying Fortresses, Dakotas, and Mustangs frequently used the runway, especially for diversions due to poor weather conditions.

Information about the landings at Carnaby from the USAAF have proved difficult to obtain. Very few archived records are to be found in the UK and obtaining them from the USA has been a fruitless search so far. The information that has been found is sadly minimal but the contribution that the Americans played during the war certainly was not! Without their help and support Britain would have struggled to win the war at all. It is a debt that is still being re-paid.

The following information is all that is known of the landings by the USSAF at Carnaby during the war. Some of the information is from the Operations Record Book and some has been provided by the Eighth Air Force Historical Society.

The USSAF

29th July 1944

On the 29th July 1944 at 15.20 a Lightning E fighter plane piloted by Lt Col Woods, USA, landed at Carnaby due to being short of fuel. He was on escort duty to protect bombers heading to the oilfields in Germany and the airfields of France. Over 1,200 heavy bombers headed over Europe, escorted by 755 fighters. Their targets were to bomb the synthetic oil plants in Merseburg/Leuna, Bremen/Oslebshausen in Germany, and Juvincourt airfield and Laon/Couvron airfield in France. Seventeen bombers and seven fighters from the USAAF were lost during that raid.

22nd August 1944

One Harvand II of USAAF was lost and landed at Carnaby due to shortage of fuel.

16th December 1944

One Fortress from 384th Bombardment Squadron, stationed at AAF 106, at Grafton Underwood landed at Carnaby, having been diverted from its base due to bad weather. The crew had been assigned a mission to bomb Bremen in Germany but due to the weather conditions that day the operation was cancelled. On their return they were diverted to Carnaby. The Captain of this aircraft was First Lieutenant Oakley H Jackson, and his crew were 2nd Lt John B Calking, 1st Lt, Leonard R Lucas, Sgt Keith R Haight, S/Sgt Paul Sanchuck, S/Sgt Allen K Ziner, T/Sgt Castano T Cappiello, Sgt James M Phelps and Sgt Vincent J Kelly.

22nd December 1944

All missions for the Eighth Air Forces were cancelled this day, however, it is recorded in Carnaby's ORB that 13 Fortresses landed at Carnaby between the hours of 12.20 and 14.10, all on diversion from their usual airbase at RAF Alconbury. The Fortresses were assigned to 812th, 813th, 814th Bombardment Squadrons (Pathfinder), assigned to the 482nd Bombardment Group (Provisional). They were flown by Capt Hermansen, 1st Lt Buckner, 1st Lt Rolin, 1st Lt Sellon, 1st Lt Oswald, 1st Lt Jason, 1st Lt MacManus, 1st Lt Smith, 1st Lt Gale, Capt Sanderson, Capt Connery, Capt Haverty and 1st Lt Granakos.

According to research carried out by 8th Air Force Historical Society, these aircraft had recently flown in from the USA via Prestwick Airport bound for RAF Alconbury. They were forming a new pathfinder squadron, Squadron No 482. The crew of these aircraft were all officers (pilots, co-pilots and navigators) and were diverted to Carnaby due to fog. Their aircraft were specially equipped with AN/APS-15 bombing and navigation radar (known as H2X by the British and "Mickey" by the USAAF) for poor weather missions. That day they were on a radar navigation training exercise.

2nd January 1945

Two Mosquitoes from USAAF landed at Carnaby on diversion at 06.20. These fighters had been protecting squadrons of bombers heading to West Germany to attack communications and tactical targets such as marshalling yards and railways. Over 1,000 bombers and 500 fighters were dispatched. Four bombers and three fighters were lost during this raid.

Chapter 8
The Post War Years

As the end of hostilities in Europe came to a close, the role of Carnaby airfield changed and continued to change over the next few decades. The first change to occur happened on the 7th May 1945 when No 4 Group handed over its airfields to Transport Command. Aircraft continued to land at Carnaby but not in the volumes that it had previously seen. Transport Command were given the task of repatriating troops from India back to the UK and wanted Carnaby as its first choice for diversions. The arrival of No 10 GCA Unit in November 1945 was to oversee the disbandment of the Station. In this time, approximately 2,000 aircraft had used the runway for practicing their landings.

After, 1st July 1946, it was agreed by both the Bridlington Council and the Air Ministry to rename RAF Carnaby to that of RAF Bridlington (Bridlington ITW had now been disbanded). However, a combination of a reduction in workload and a lack of manpower made it difficult to keep Carnaby operational, and as such on the 20th October 1946 Carnaby (RAF Bridlington) was finally closed.

A year later, in September 1947, the airfield was in use again by Blackburns. This time the airfield would be used for trials of prototype aircraft. However, this was short lived and by December the same year Transport Command declared they would no longer be using the site. Care of the site was given to 25 Group Flying Training Command at Driffield.

A period of uncertainly surrounded Carnaby for several months until a new flying school, 203 Advanced Flying School, was established at Driffield in September 1949 to fly Vampires and Meteors. Carnaby (now RAF Bridlington) would be used on a limited basis for circuit and landing training by Meteor pilots as the long runway was ideal for practise training runs. The runway itself had to be remarked and moved 500 yards westward to enable the road to remain open during use. For a brief period, 203 moved their aircraft to Carnaby whilst the runway at Driffield was resurfaced.

Blackburn landing at a local airfield in East Yorkshire.

In May 1950, Blackburn requested to use Carnaby (RAF Bridlington) for prototypes trials. The first set of trials were for the GAL 60, Universal Freighter, WF320 and then later on to trial research aircraft, the Handley Page HP88. Testing was carried out on a new crescent shaped wing planned for use on Victors. The HP88 was moved by road from Brough to Carnaby and re-assembled in a blister hangar. Several test flights successfully took place at Carnaby and then the aircraft was moved to Standstead. Unfortunately, during further high speed trials the aircraft broke up and was completely destroyed.

Carnaby was no stranger to crash landings but as aircraft became faster and more advanced, the crashes became more serious, with two fatalities. The first post war crash that is known occurred on the 20th December 1951 when two Meteor Mk 4's crashed at Carnaby. Meteor VT280, flown by a pupil pilot, crashed when one engine flamed out whilst doing circuit training. The pilot lost control and the aircraft stalled. It crashed when coming in to land. The pilot escaped with injuries. The second crash involved a Meteor RA 426. It collided with another Meteor (WW304) whilst heading for this relief landing ground. The pupil pilot bailed out safely leaving the aircraft to crash to the south of the airfield. The precise location of the crash site is not known. A year later, on the 16th September 1952, there was a third crash at Carnaby. A Meteor Mk 4 (VT127) also from 203 AFS, Driffield, smashed into the ground whilst practising aeronautics. The pilot was killed and one person on the ground was decapitated. The following year, on the 18th May 1954, another Meteor, MK8 (WE879) from Leconfield crashed. It lost its leading edge of one of its wings whilst in flight. The reasons for this are not known. The pilot made a belly landing but the aircraft was damaged beyond repair.

In the early 1950's the USAF became interested in Carnaby. They wanted a base in the UK for a Fighter Escort Wing of approximately 75 aircraft. During the start of any hostilities, this unit would move to the

UK. Their purpose was to escort B36 bombers during operations in wartime. The USAF requested that the runway be strengthened using several inches of concrete and asphalt, high intensity lighting to be installed and for the provision of sick quarters. To house their staff they required accommodation for 25 officers, 34 SNCOs and 272 Cpls & A/Cs. They also requested a scaled quota of married quarters.

For the safety of the Station and aircrews, the USAF planned to install fire tender bays close to the existing Control Tower, provide 48 hard standing areas and more fuel storage tanks to add to the 168,000 imperial gallons that could already be stored there. The following equipment would also be a necessity, 2 ambulances (one heavy, one light), 2 x 10 cwt cars, one passenger car, 1 x12 cwt van, 1 x 1 ton truck, 1 x 3 ton truck, 1 x ww medium aircraft tractor, heavy crane, 4 x 2,500 gallons refuellers, 1 x 950 gallons G&O refueller, 4 fire trucks, 2 snow clearance trucks, 1 ATC trailer and 1 land-mark beacon trailer. The work at Carnaby commenced in 1955 after the RAF had left and was expected to cost approximately £1,000,000 to £1,500,000.

For a brief time, Fighter Command also became interested in this site and discussed the possibility of a joint venture with the USAF but due to budget constraints the RAF soon gave up this idea. Two years later the US Air Force halted their progress, informing the Air Ministry that it did not intend to complete this project.

In October 1958, the RAF and USAF established a joint venture under the code name "Project Emily". Carnaby was to become a THOR missile base. THOR missiles were front line intermediate range ballistic missiles. They were tall white missiles, each armed with a nuclear warhead which could be aimed as far away as 1,500 miles. Carnaby was officially handed back to Bomber Command on the 24th October 1958, and once again, Driffield was its parent base.

On the 1st August, No 150 Squadron, a Strategic Missile Squadron, took over the running of Carnaby under the control of No 1 Group. It was one of five units which made up the Driffield Complex. As Carnaby had few permanent buildings, specially built trailers were brought in to be utilised as workshops. As this was a joint venture, both the British and US governments agreed that the missiles could only be launched when both governments agreed to do so. To protect this agreement there was a special procedure in place whereby a set of twin keys would have to be used simultaneously in order to fire the missiles. The keys were held by senior RAF and USAF officers respectively.

Each Strategic Missile Squadron had three THOR launch pads and No 150 Squadron were responsible for LE's 37, 38, and 39. To protect these sites it was thought that conventional aircraft would be of limited use. It was therefore decided that surface to air missiles would be needed instead. The Bloodhound I was the chosen weapon. These surface to air missiles could reach a speed in excess of Mach 2 and had a range of approximately 50 miles. Bloodhound sites were normally situated close to the THOR missiles but not usually on the same site for fear that one may fall on the THOR missile itself. However, Carnaby was the exception and the Bloodhound I missiles, manned by 247 Squadron, were located on the same site. This was because of its vulnerability to surprise attacks by low flying aircraft. There were two clusters of 16 launch pads, each with its own Launch Control Post and a Sting Ray target illuminating radar.

Security was an absolute priority at THOR Sites and in April 1961 two operations' officers arrived at Carnaby to train up Air Defence Operators who had recently arrived. Security was further tightened during the Cuban Missile Crisis in 1962 but a year later the USAF withdrew their support for THOR missiles as it was thought that they were too vulnerable to surprise enemy attack. The Bloodhound control system had been taken over by the Master Radar station at Patrington in January just before the Anglo-American agreement came to an end. The THOR missile launch pads were dissembled and taken back to America and the Station was handed over to Driffield, resulting in the ultimate disbanding of No 150 Squadron. The Bloodhound I also came to an end as evidence showed it was flawed and often jammed, leading to the disbandment of No 247 Squadron and the scrapping of missiles. The RAF then took over the defence role again with its V Bomber force. The site at Carnaby was cleared and by the end of 1963 lay dormant again. RAF Bempton took control of the care and maintenance of the site but by the end of February 1964 the site was handed over to RAF Leconfield.

Discussions were held in 1966 about using Carnaby as a Relief Landing Ground for a Flying Training Unit but after further deliberations this idea was abandoned. It then lay disused for a number of years before being sold to joint owners, Bridlington Corporation and Bridlington RDC, for the sum of £50,000. An industrial estate was gradually built up over a few years but for a short while light aircraft were still able to land at the west end. Also, for a brief period of time, motor racing events were held there but gradually ceased. Now the site is well developed with several large units and many smaller units. Its fortunes have fluctuated over the years due to the ebb and flow of the local economy. The Control Tower has long since been dismantled and in its place stands a large lake which is used by the local motor boat club. Some post war buildings still remain. The barracks which were built after the war were used for a short time as temporary shops for small businesses but have now been converted into flats. The officers' houses have been turned into residential houses, and the hospital and mortuary have been pulled down.

It is easy to pass by the old runway now without a second glance. The history of the airfield could soon be lost if nothing is done to mark its existence. Road names, such as Lancaster Road and Wellington Way reflect the aircraft that once landed here in large numbers. A small granite block erected in 2014 with the inscription "In memory of Carnaby (Bridlington) Airfield, Opened 26.3.1944, Closed 1967, Dedicated to all units and personnel based here" is all that marks the spot!

This book therefore hopes to keep the history and memory alive of all those who worked, served and landed here. Monies raised from this book will help fund a befitting memorial to mark the contribution and the sacrifices that were made by so many, for future generations to come.

Appendix
Roll of Honour
Carnaby Crew

Date	Number	Name	Initials	Rank	Notes
28.03.44		Wood	CP	F/Lt	Medical Officer
02.04.44	37526	Fowle DFC	FRC	W/Cdre	Station Commander
10.05.44	106043	Hemelik	A	F/Lt	F/Control duties
10.05.44	72692	Lea	SFB	F/Lt	F/C Duties
21.06.44	104157	Corson	GA	F/O	
26.06.44	110049	Strong	A	S/L	To command 2833 AA Squadron
27.06.44	134772	Ambridge	GEC	F/O	
29.06.44	118113	Cameron	J	S/L	
08.06.44	1358226	Stephenson	GW	Sgt	Mentioned in despatches London Gazette
08.06.44	2215751	Cludnay	A	Cpl	Mentioned in despatches London Gazette
08.06.44	134782	Bramwell	AE	F/O	
08.06.44	149415	Moorhouse		F/O	Signals duties
08.06.44	119046	Raine	FW	F/O	
08.06.44	141241	Dungate	CHJ	F/O	CWF Duties
14.07.44	85959	Glosssop	C		
14.07.44	108698	Franklin	WH	F/O	
14.07.44	104157	Conson	GA	F/O	
14.07.44	114967	Taylor	R	F/O	
14.07.44	134772	Ambridge	GEC	F/O	
14.07.44	171255	Tait	JW	P/O	
01.09.44	155294	Bell	JL	F/O	Posted for flying control duties
18.10.44		Hurley (RCAF)	F	S/L	took command of the station
15.10.44	161581	Armstrong	L	F/O	Technical (signals) duties
15.10.44	149415	Moorhouse	B	F/O	Technical (signals) duties
17.10.44	1604624	Henshaw	AJ	F/Sgt	Aircrew reception duties, posted from 51 Squadron
17.10.44	1835982	Morris	T	Sgt	Aircrew reception duties, posted from 51 Squadron
17.10.44	1215094	Scars	R	Sgt	Aircrew reception duties, posted from 51 Squadron
08.11.44	185743	Freeman	DH	P/O	Aircrew reception duties
14.11.44	185127	Morris	T	P/O	Aircrew reception duties
01.12.44	Aus 176	Scott (RAAF)	WWG	W/Cmdr	Took command of the station
01.01.45	68269	Jolly	H	F/Lt	Defence training duties
22.01.45	42283	Viney DSO DFC	JM	W/Cmdr	took command of the station (640 Squadron)
22.01.45	51413	Wilkie	JCT	F/O	Tech (Eng) duties

Date	Number	Name	Initials	Rank	Notes
22.01.45	49502	Major	CR	P/O	Tech (Eng) duties
31.01.45	184496	Brown	AJ	F/O	From 578 Squadron
01.02.45	417147	Willington	AF	P/O	Flying duties
01.02.45	428797	Sanderson	RW	F/O	Flying duties
20.02.45	3006461	Chamberlain	SJ	Sgt	N/O duties
26.02.45	84556	Hiscock	WG	F/Lt	For intelligence duties
26.02.45	183967	Burhart	L	P/O	For intelligence duties from RAF Snaith
05.03.45	148648	McQueen	RP	F/O	For duty as M/T Officer
05.03.45	1604234	Tufton	H	F/Sgt	Posted from 100 Sqdn for aircrew reception duties
12.03.45	1230541	Windsor	JH	W/O	For M/T duties
16.03.45	132395	Meade	RWC	F/L	For Flying control duties
28.03.45	186137	Morris	T	P/O	Posted to 158 Squadron
28.03.45	1215094	Sears	RG	F/Sgt	Posted to 158 Squadron
01.04.45	1823108	Whitson	RK	Sgt	Aircrew reception duties
04.04.45	936516	Neafsey	TR	F/Sgt	Aircrew reception duties
04.04.45	1042199	Winton	WJ	Sgt	Aircrew reception duties
06.04.45	122033	Hill	F	F/O	Posted from RAF Station Foulsham
24.04.45	1604642	Henshaw	AJ	F/Sgt	Posted to 102 Squadron
29.04.45	185743	Freeman	DM	F/O	Posted to 57 Squadron, 2nd tour of duty
01.01.45	118657	Lally	R	F/Lt	Aircrew reception duties
01.01.45	154084	Beach	M	F/O	Aircrew reception duties
01.01.45	187470	Aldous	CJ	P/O	
03.01.45	1895494	Day	LN	F/S	Posted from RAF Station Weeton
05.05.45	196058	Foster	R	P/O	Aircrew reception duties
04.05.45		Hobbs	J	F/Lt	CTBA from 43 Base
14.05.45	82373	Rogers DFC	EB	F/Lt	For admin duties
14.05.45		Schofield	FH	S/Ldr	Posted to RAF Station Melbourne
03.06.45	138354	Briscoe	HB	F/L	From 43 Base
03.06.45	150604	Botte	J	F/L	From 51 Squadron
03.06.45	139641	Vollum	R	F/Lt	
03.06.45	425927	Murray	BR	F/O	
06.06.45	86279	Franklin	JB	F/Lt	
24.06.45	75866	Nelson	H	S/Ldr	Posted to 100 PDC
09.07.45	183967	Burkhart	L	P/O	Posted to 229 Group
12.07.45	190830	Lawson	EW	P/O	Posted to 51 Squadron
02.08.45	101233	Bowyer	WM	P/O	Posted to 100 PDC
09.08.45	108361	Field	GH	F/O	Posted to RAF Station Manston
09.08.45	101201	Watson	FC	F/O	
15.08.45	957660	Bishop	EM	Sgt	
18.08.45	1310766	Bishop	JB	F/Sgt	
01.09.45	57480	Newitt	BF	F/O	Posted to 158 Squadron
04.09.45	146244	Thompson	E	F/O	Posted from RAF Lissett for flying control duties
07.09.45	125581	Stanyard DFC	LF	F/L	Attached from RAF Holm

Date	Number	Name	Initials	Rank	Notes
08.09.45		O'Hara	FJ	F/Sgt	
08.09.45		Johnson	M	W/O	
22.09.45	56971	Dellbridge	FJ	F/O	*attached from Ricall for signals duties*
23.09.45	1540321	Beach	M	F/O	*Posted to HQFC*
25.09.45	1865650	Rush		Sgt	
18.09.45	129976	Smith	L	F/Lt	
18.09.45	115336	Haigh	DA	F/Lt	
18.09.45	174759	Smth	PJ	P/O	
18.09.45	570981	Cooper	JG	W/O	
18.09.45	749379	Lawrence	J	W/O	
01.10.45	72910	Pairman	JR	F/Lt	
04.10.45	139042	Glass	H	F/O	
04.10.45	84556	Hiscox	WG	F/Lt	
22.10.45	103954	Redfern	J	F/O	
24.10.45	43867	Cuff	ER	F/O	
08.11.45	169866	Larkins	AT	F/O	
11.11.45	1865465	Gill		Sgt	
12.11.45	1798431	Lanigan	M	F/Sgt	
14.11.45	1621546	Boyes		F/Sgt	
16.11.45	37547	Stewart	JB	W/Cdre	
20.11.45	1594871	Stalley		F/Sgt	
20.11.45	1812628	Ainsworth		Sgt	
01.12.45	1079583	Bannister	A	W/O	
01.12.45	1197832	Peplow	VW	W/O	
01.12.45	1684536	Proctor		Sgt	
01.12.45	1097016	Parkin		F/Sgt	
05.12.45	1378654	Watchorn		W/O	
06.12.45	1811601	Milkins		Sgt	
06.12.45	1814624	Kemp		Sgt	
06.12.45	1576086	Hyslop		F/Sgt	
06.12.45	1622307	Holcroft		W/O	
06.12.45	2255459	Wark		F/Sgt	
06.12.45	1597835	Wildsmith		F/Sgt	
06.12.45	2209545	Bass		Sgt	
06.12.45	3005541	Hills		Sgt	
10.12.45	1819060	Fetherston		Sgt	
10.12.45	1836501	Shaw	L	Sgt	
12.12.45	1578562	Dorbett		F/Sgt	
12.12.45	1667721	Sugden	WJ	F/Sgt	
12.12.45	1677081	Brown	TE	F/Sgt	
13.12.45	1895853	Nicholson		W/O	
13.12.45	2220345	Roberts		F/Sgt	
18.12.45	74217	Richmond	JCT	A/S/Ldr	*station admin officer*
18.12.45	1774018	Owat		F/Sgt	

Date	Number	Name	Initials	Rank	Notes
27.12.45	1899658	Parry-Maddocks		Sgt	
27.12.45	85837	Ryan	GWP	F/Lt	
02.01.46	1582932	Slater	HA	F/Sgt	
03.01.46	1898015	Parker	BH	Sgt	
04.01.46	169269	Wade	VL	F/Lt	
09.01.46	57671	Cooper	JG	P/O	
09.01.46	201847	Lawrence	GH	P/O	
09.01.46	959589	King		W/O	
10.01.46	1578562	Corbett		F/Sgt	
14.01.46	1581188	Wilson		F/Sgt	
19.01.46	1821811	Kay		Sgt	
20.01.46	1321301	Newman		F/Sgt	
24.01.46	1865650	Ruck		F/Sgt	
27.01.46	81373	Pugh	DW	F/Lt	
31.01.46	158445	Sullivan	WT	P/O	
31.01.46	908879	Gibbs	EA	W/O	
02.02.46	1606780	Harty		F/Sgt	
03.02.46		Hayden	TA	F/O	
22.02.46	1787584	Brown		F/S	
04.03.46	1384505	Alderton		F/S	
05.03.46	1590876	Clayton		F/S	
14.03.46	56811	Clarke	E	F/O	
16.03.46	174063	Franklin	DWN	F/O	
25.03.46	131993	Wilton	RJS	F/Lt	
25.03.46	175973	Bullock	EG	F/O	
		Yates	Bernard	Bombadier	Training in aircraft recognition

10 Squadron

Date	Name	Initials	Rank	Notes
07.03.45	Poley	E	W/O	
	Spratt	R	Sgt	
	Johnson	A	F/Sgt	
	Hebden		F/Sgt	
	Cohen	M	W/O	
	Speight	R	Sgt	
	Grayson	R	F/Sgt	

42 Squadron

Date	Name	Initials	Rank	Notes
28.02.44	Jones	GI	F/L	Halifax ME 952 "I" Lack of brake pressure

51 Squadron

Date	Name	Initials	Rank	Notes
03.09.44	Coldrick	IC	F/O	Halifax III
	Markham	G	P/O	MH "A"
	Rounce	MH	Sgt	MZ348
	Dobson (Aus)	RJ	F/S	Diverted due to weather
	Butterfield	FS	Sgt	
	Lea	WJ	Sgt	
	Bowes	H	Sgt	
03.09.44	Willis	WE	F/O	Halifax III
	Vaight	DH	Sgt	MH "B"
	Philpott	GE	Sgt	MZ319
	Polden	FH	Sgt	Diverted due to weather
	Howard	BC	Sgt	
	Burgess	WF	Sgt	
	Davies	AH	Sgt	
03.09.44	Robertson	GM	F/L	Halifax III
	Jones (Aus)	RF	F/S	MH "C"
	Franklin	GE	F/S	MZ 851
	Terry	TW	F/S	Diverted due to weather
	Frear	EG	Sgt	
	Page	PA	Sgt	
	Dent	E	F/S	

Date	Name	Initials	Rank	Notes
03.09.44	Boyers	RH	F/O	Halifax III
	Russell	T	Sgt	MH "D"
	Bachelder (Can)	LR	F/O	MZ 767
	Ballinger	PI	P/O	Diverted due to weather
	Jenkins	HR	Sgt	
	Blamire	OH	Sgt	
	Fry	JG	Sgt	
03.09.44	Longmore	W	F/O	Halifax III
	Hamar (Can)	LM	W/O	MH "E"
	McKnight	RC	F/S	MZ 765
	Holloway	F	F/S	Diverted due to weather
	Mullett	PJR	Sgt	
	Godfrey	GW	Sgt	
	Talbot	W	Sgt	
03.09.44	Abell	RE	F/S	Halifax III
	Marsh	EI	Sgt	MH "H"
	Mowat	DD	Sgt	MZ 868
	White (Aus)	JE	F/S	Diverted due to weather
	Morrill	DA	Sgt	
	Rouse	DH	Sgt	
	Jones	PO	Sgt	
03.09.44	Norton (Can)	LR	F/O	Halifax III
	Perry	KF	F/S	MH "K"
	Murphy (Can)	R	F/S	NA 493
	Duff	WJH	F/S	Diverted due to weather
	Bullock	EG	P/O	
	Hope	R	Sgt	
	Cran	J	F/S	
03.09.44	Hopkins	H	S/L	Halifax III
	McMath (Can)	J	F/O	MH "L"
	Nicol	MB	F/O	NA 496
	Brownrigg	OG	Sgt	Diverted due to weather
	Williamson	W	Sgt	
	Staples	PG	F/O	
	Judd	KF	Sgt	

Date	Name	Initials	Rank	Notes
03.09.44	Mitchell	KF	F/S	Halifax III
	Stokes	CD	Sgt	MH "M"
	Clark	JF	Sgt	LK 844
	Lumsden	A	Sgt	Diverted due to weather
	Morris	AE	Sgt	
	Ford	RA	Sgt	
	Carass	TW	Sgt	
03.09.44	Collyer	CT	F/O	Halifax III
	Brandon	AG	F/O	MH "N"
	Pollitt	W	Sgt	NZ 624
	Standfield	EP	F/S	Diverted due to weather
	Gartland	J	Sgt	
	Popple	LA	Sgt	
	Delaney	DT	P/O	
03.09.44	Gardner	JC	Sgt	Halifax III
	Lofthouse	FC	Sgt	MH "O"
	Ward	JH	Sgt	MZ 916
	Hoskin	DH	Sgt	Diverted due to weather
	Parry	C	Sgt	
	Hodson	JA	Sgt	
	Eyre	A	Sgt	
03.09.44	Bischoff	JN	F/O	Halifax III
	Steifel	PG	Sgt	MH "P"
	Plested	JO	F/S	LK 751
	Jones	LJ	Sgt	Diverted due to weather
	Joyce	N	Sgt	
	Watson	BA	F/S	
	Page	IC	F/S	
03.09.44	Binns	H	F/O	Halifax III
	Mes	JA	Sgt	MH "R"
	Kidd	E	F/O	MZ 917
	Rudd	CE	F/S	Diverted due to weather
	Treadwell	A	Sgt	
	Buchanan	C	Sgt	
	Kemp	JB	Sgt	

Date	Name	Initials	Rank	Notes
03.09.44	Potts	K	W/O	Halifax III
	Frew	RG	F/S	MH "V"
	Hobbs	DA	F/S	MZ 758
	Patey	WG	F/S	Diverted due to weather
	McGowan	L	Sgt	
	Hill	GJ	Sgt	
	Howard	SM	Sgt	
03.09.44	Stone	HM	F/O	Halifax III
	Thomas	KC	JF/O	MH "W"
	Coutts	HA	JF/O	MZ 933
	Wyatt	JA	Sgt	Diverted due to weather
	Stuart	S	Sgt	
	Ferme	AW	Sgt	
	Baker	MP	Sgt	
03.09.44	Kelly (Aus)	AJ	F/S	Halifax III
	Willie (Aus)	JR	F/S	MH "X"
	Lodge	RB	Sgt	LV 832
	Wynn (Aus)	RC	F/S	Diverted due to weather
	Strange	N	Sgt	
	Sauls	T	Sgt	
	Cunningham	AG	Sgt	
03.09.44	Berry	L	F/S	Halifax III
	Hinchcliffe	P	Sgt	MH "Y"
	Cantle	AB	F/S	LV 865
	Davies	J	Sgt	Diverted due to weather
	Williams	N	Sgt	
	Heseltine	RA	Sgt	
	Gunning	EC	Sgt	
03.09.44	Popplewell	EM	P/O	Halifax III
	Johns	DE	Sgt	MH "Z"
	Hissette Can)	A	Sgt	LW 820
	Muddiman	A	Sgt	Diverted due to weather
	Hunter	AW	Sgt	
	Boydell	RA	Sgt	
	Annis	K	Sgt	

Date	Name	Initials	Rank	Notes
03.09.44	Faulkner (Aus)	AL	F/O	Halifax III
	Miller (Aus)	RB	P/O	C6 "B"
	Maritz	GS	P/O	LW 461
	Johnston	H	F/S	Diverted due to weather
	Capeling	H	Sgt	
	Watts	GE	Sgt	
	George	TP	F/S	

57 Squadron

Date	Name	Initials	Rank	Notes
16.11.44	Jackson	J	F/O	Lancaster I LL 940
	Dack	J	Sgt	Landed at Carnaby
	Wilson	J	F/S	Reason unknown
	McLure	G	F/S	
	Hibbard	L	F/S	
	Burrows	J	Sgt	
	Crighton	J	Sgt	

58 Squadron

Date	Name	Initials	Rank	Notes
08.03.45	Lawson	RN	F/O	JP 350
	Ricketts	J	F/Sgt	Abandoned sortie owing to
	Kohler (Aus)	CH	P/O	starboard tyre bursting on take-
	Blades	RE	W/O	off - diverted to Carnaby
	Yeandle	FC	F/Sgt	
	Smith	JF	F/Sgt	
	Magness	KW	F/Sgt	
	Costello (Can)	PC	F/O	
	Jones	V E	F/O	

79

Date	Name	Initials	Rank	Notes
08.04.45	Lawson	RN	F/Lt	Halifax PN 425
	Ricketts	J	F/Sgt	Badly damaged by flak
	Kohler (Aus)	CH	P/O	Mid upper gunner
	Magness	WL	F/Sgt	blown out of aircraft
	Blades	RE	W/O	Found hanging beneath aircraft
	Yeandle	FC	F/Sgt	alive and still smiling
	Smith	W	F/O	
	Smith	JF	F/Sgt	
	Jones	V	F/O	

76 Squadron

Date	Name	Initials	Rank	Notes
06.07.44	Mottram	LA	P/O	Halifax III
	Hill	BG	Sgt	ME 732 "D"
	Lincoln	GE	F/S	Undercarriage would not
	Phillips	BH	Sgt	lock
	Caseman	KH	Sgt	Crash landed at
	Walden	JR	Sgt	Carnaby
	Burch	W	Sgt	
16.11.44				2 aircraft landed
				details unknown
05.12.44	Callaghan	TC	F/LT	Halifax III
	Mason	NF	Sgt	MZ 967 "N"
	Ward	JS	F/O	"Y" Type
	Stadnyk	A	F/O	Hydraulics trouble
	Colquhoun	RA	F/Sgt	landed at Carnaby
	Cooper	WH	F/Sgt	
	Cragg	AC	F/Sgt	
21.12.44				3 aircraft landed
				details unknown

Date	Name	Initials	Rank	Notes
29.12.44	Ball	HL	F/S	Halifax III
	Phillips	WJ	F/S	LL 554 "A"
	Mallen	WB	F/O	Engine trouble
	Boydell	E	F/S	landed at Carnaby
	Pennington	JM	F/S	
	Faulkner	JM	Sgt	
	McNeill	J	F/S	
	Furness	E	F/O	
07.01.45				1 aircraft landed details unknown
02.02.45				1 aircraft landed details unknown
27.02.45	Inglis	KB	F/Lt	Halifax III
	Thompson	J	P/O	NA 584 "F"
	Buchanan	J	P/O	landed at Carnaby
	Hogg	DM	P/O	
	Gibbs	JA	F/S	
	Dallison	SN	Sgt	
	Snook	RW	P/O	
03.03.45	Oleynik (RCAF)	P	P/O	
	Firmin	HC	Sgt	
	MacMillan	DG	F/Sgt	
	Menard (RCAF)	JD	WO	
	Freeman	RJ	F/S	
	Maltby (RCAF)	WT	F/Sgt	
	MacDougal	RC	F/Sgt	
09.04.45				1 aircraft landed details unknown
08.06.45				1 aircraft landed details unknown

77 Squadron

Date	Name	Initials	Rank	Notes
01.06.44	Morrison (CAN)	JD	F/O	Halifax III
	Moodie	A	Sgt	MZ 694 "G"
	Melvin (CAN)	TJ	Sgt	landed at Carnaby
	Dye (CAN)	JE	P/O	
	Johnson (CAN)	FA	F/S	
	Puchalski (CAN)	A	Sgt	
	Macritchie (CAN)	MD	Sgt	
	Holliday	MD	F/O	
08/09.06.44	Bird (AUS)	HW	P/O	Halifax III
	Castle-Hall	RA	Sgt	NA 508 "A"
	Freemantle	AB	Sgt	Diverted to Carnaby
	McKay (AUS)	SW	F/O	
	Warren (AUS)	RJ	F/S	
	Lauder	JA	Sgt	
	Meeghan	FA	F/S	
08/09.06.44	Jakeman (CAN)	CI	P/O	Halifax III
	Manstoff	A	Sgt	NA 532 "E"
	West	RJ	P/O	landed at Carnaby
	Giles	FL	F/S	
	Hargreaves	JW	F/S	
	Steed(CAN)	RJ	F/O	
	McFadden (CAN)	RJJ	F/S	
08/09.06.44	Smith	H	P/O	Halifax III
	Gunn	SM	Sgt	NA 524 "F"
	Jacques	HV	F/S	Landed at Carnaby
	Fisher	R	F/S	
	Norwood	GT	Sgt	
	Cranswick	A	Sgt	
	Roddy	TA	Sgt	
08/09.06.44	Jewell	R	P/O	Halifax III
	Smith	JJ	Sgt	MZ 699 "K"
	Holmes	WC	F/S	Landed at Carnaby
	Mcleod	C	F/S	
	Hall	P	Sgt	
	Boulding	RJ	Sgt	
	Conroy	BP	Sgt	

Date	Name	Initials	Rank	Notes
08/09.06.44	Pearce	HV	P/O	Halifax III
	Archbold	F	Sgt	MX 697 "L"
	Kendall	GB	F/S	Landed at Carnaby
	Edwards	CGF	F/S	
	Morgan	FE	F/S	
	Brooks	R	F/S	
	Hancocks DFM	ID	Sgt	
08/09.06.44	Lord	FE	F/O	Halifax III
	Fox	TW	Sgt	MX 700 "O"
	Farmer	AJ	F/O	Landed at Carnaby
	Page	WC	F/O	
	Erasmuson	RH	P/O	
	Allen	R	Sgt	
	Barker	WA	Sgt	
08/09.06.44	Beadle	CH	P/O	Halifax III
	White	C	Sgt	MX 705 "Q"
	Williams	R	F/O	Landed at Carnaby
	Sinclair	PG	F/O	
	Ninmo		Sgt	
	Mearsdon	C	Sgt	
	Robertston	FH	Sgt	
08/09.06.44	Thompson	AG	Sgt	Halifax III
	Coates	W	Sgt	MZ 715 "Z"
	Hoar (CAN)	AM	F/O	Landed at Carnaby
	Haggary	CL	Sgt	
	Dade	AW	Sgt	
	Taylor	AF	Sgt	
	Salmons	RH	Sgt	
08/09.06.44	Hale (AFC)	EJ	F/L	Halifax III
	Mann	AK	Sgt	MZ 704 "P"
	Varley	RMG	F/S	Landed at Carnaby
	Cooper	MG	F/O	
	Hull	AFR	Sgt	
	Bird (AUS)		F/S	
	Parry	CF	Sgt	

Date	Name	Initials	Rank	Notes
16/17.06.44	Brown	VR	F/S	Halifax III
	Thomas	C	Sgt	MZ 673 "B"
	Quarry	J	Sgt	Crash landed at Carnaby
	Smoothy	AG	Sgt	No hydraulics
	Jennings	AA	F/S	
	Bouvet	A	Sgt	
	Smith	JJ	Sgt	
16/17.06.44	Welch	WJJ	S/Ldr	Halifax III
	Corden	DW	P/O	MZ 739 "W"
	Dean	JEH	P/O	landed at Carnaby
	Masson	JE	F/S	
	Edwards	EV	F/S	
	May	CGK	F/S	
	Sutton	E	F/S	
24.06.44	Brown	VR	F/S	Halifax III
	Thomas	C	Sgt	MZ 694 "G"
	Quarry	J	Sgt	landed at Carnaby
	Smoothy	AG	Sgt	
	Jennings (AUS)	AA	F/S	
	Bouvet	A	Sgt	
	Smith	JJ	Sgt	
28/29.06.44	Morison (CAN)	JD	F/O	Halifax III
	Moodie	A	Sgt	MZ 694 "G"
	Melvin (CAN)	TJ	Sgt	landed at Carnaby
	Steward	RA	Sgt	
	Johnson (CAN)	FA	F/S	
	Puchalski (CAN)	A	Sgt	
	Macritchie (CAN)	MD	Sgt	
17/18.08.44	Jury	K	F/O	Halifax III
	Stonham	CD	P/O	MZ 769 "R"
	Christian (CAN)	JC	P/O	Landed at Carnaby due
	Hall (CAN)	EK	W/O	to tail wheel failed to show down
	Mash	TE	F/S	over base
	McGillivray	CD	Sgt	
	Craig	A	F/S	

Date	Name	Initials	Rank	Notes
17/18.08.44	Brown	VR	F/S	Halifax III
	Thomas	C	Sgt	NA 525 "D"
	Quarry	J	Sgt	landed at Carnaby
	Smoothy	AG	Sgt	
	Jennings (AUS)	AA	F/S	
	Bouvet	A	Sgt	
	Smith	JJ	Sgt	
23.10.44	Ward	E	F/O	Halifax III
	Pearce	RAC	Sgt	MZ 396 "J"
	Anderson	JA	Sgt	landed at Carnaby
	Kerr	TM	F/S	
	Devis	SG	F/S	
	Dyke	J	Sgt	
	Edwards	WJ	Sgt	
16.11.44	Fitzgerald	P	F/O	Halfiax III
	Carter	A	Sgt	MZ 353 "C"
	Bicknell	KJA	F/S	Landed at Carnaby
	Parsons	EJ	F/S	
	Overett	AC	Sgt	
	Pickering	JM	Sgt	
	Meekinson	P	Sgt	
16.11.44	Fitzharris	SJ	F/O	Halifax III
	Stockley	F	Sgt	MZ 708 "E"
	Melvin	TJ	W/O	Landed at Carnaby
	Shuker	D	F/O	due to no brake pressure
	Stewart	TL	F/O	
	Hannah	EJ	Sgt	
	Wassell	RB	Sgt	
21.12.44	Gaddes (NZ)	JM	F/S	Halifax III
	Thompson	KW	Sgt	Mz 967 "N"
	Hobbs	JT	F/S	landed at Carnaby
	Bullen	PG	F/S	
	Chapman	FN	F/S	
	Nash	LJ	F/S	
	Weaire	EL	Sgt	

Date	Name	Initials	Rank	Notes
21.12.44	Thomson	FI	F/Lt	Halifax III
	Snow	ES	Sgt	MZ 803 "G"
	Embree	AT	P/O	Diverted To Carnaby
	Miller	JL	W/O	
	Austin	G	F/S	
	Harper	JH	F/S	
	Ford	NR	F/S	
21.12.44	Cooke	AC	F/O	Halifax III
	Hutchinson	JC	Sgt	MZ 801 "T"
	Amy	HP	F/S	Diverted To Carnaby
	Cassignol	AM	F/S	
	Baxter	TH	F/S	
	MacDonald	A	Sgt	
	Cade	JA	F/S	
21.12.44	Fitzharris	SJ	F/O	Halifax III
	Stockley	F	Sgt	MZ 708 "E"
	Dunhill	A	P/O	Diverted To Carnaby
	Shuker	D	F/O	
	Stewart	TL	F/O	
	Hannah	EJ	Sgt	
	Wassell	RB	Sgt	
	Stewart	J	W/O	
21.12.44	Tarling	E	F/O	Halifax III
	Smith	D	Sgt	MZ 346 "B"
	Brown	LL WR	W/O	Diverted to Carnaby
	Anglin	WF	F/o	
	Currie	LL WR	F/S	
	Hill	HA	F/S	
	Hopley	AW	F/S	
21.12.44	Thomson	FI	F/Lt	Halifax III
	Snow	ES	Sgt	MZ 803 "C"
	Embree	AT	P/O	Diverted to Carnaby
	Miller	JL	W/O	
	Austin	G	F/S	
	Harper	JH	F/S	
	Ford	NR	F/S	

Date	Name	Initials	Rank	Notes
21.12.44	Merlin	R	F/O	Halifax III
	Morley	GS	Sgt	MZ 354 "M"
	Bennett	RM	W/O	Diverted to Carnaby
	Robinson	JH	F/S	
	Cook	JW	F/S	
	Simmonds	R	F/S	
	Peers	W	F/S	
21.12.44	Hansen	G	F/O	Halifax III
	Forster	C	P/O	MZ 393"S"
	Morley	RE	P/O	Diverted to Carnaby
	Bairstow	A	P/O	
	Knapp	RA	F/Sgt	
	Talbot	HJ	Sgt	
	Smith	JG	Sgt	
21.12.44	King	RL	F/Lt	Halifax III
	Hindley	AJ	Sgt	MZ 353 "C"
	Joules	S	Sgt	landed at Carnaby
	Chattle	AW	F/S	
	Punt	W	F/S	
	Clayton	J	F/S	
	Smith	TW	Sgt	
21.12.44	Hurlbut	E	F/Lt	Halifax III
	Shellahear	JW	Sgt	MZ 804 "K"
	Black	S	F/S	landed at Carnaby
	Major	JFO	P/O	
	Mann	D	Sgt	
	Dobson	WR	F/S	
	Essex	CB	F/S	
21.12.44	Foot	WA	F/O	Halifax III
	Pratt	AJ	Sgt	MZ 396"J"
	Milton	D	F/O	landed at Carnaby
	Patterson	JV	F/O	
	Sutton	C	F/S	
	Dunansun	R	F/S	
	Dennehey	R	F/S	

Date	Name	Initials	Rank	Notes
24.12.44	Fitzharris	SJ	F/O	Halifax III
	Stockley	F	Sgt	MZ 708 "E"
	Dunhill	LA	P/O	landed at Carnaby
	Shuker	D	F/O	
	Stewart	TL	F/O	
	Hannah	EJ	Sgt	
	Wassell	RB	Sgt	
	Hendry	R	W/O	
26.12.44	Tarling	E	F/O	Halifax III
	Smith	D	Sgt	MZ 353 "C"
	Brownell	WP	W/O	Diverted to Carnaby
	Anglin	WF	F/o	
	Currie	LL WR	F/S	
	Hill	HA	F/S	
	Hopley	AW	F/S	
26.12.44	Hansen	G	F/O	Halifax III
	Forster	C	P/O	MZ 396 "J"
	Morley	RE	P/O	Diverted to Carnaby
	Bairstow	A	P/O	
	Knapp	RA	F/Sgt	
	Talbot	HJ	Sgt	
	Smith	JG	Sgt	
26.12.44	Brunton	L	F/O	Halifax III
	Peters	R	Sgt	MZ 809 "U"
	Hafso	SO	F/S	Diverted to Carnaby
	Counahan	PF	F/S	
	Baker	AE	F/S	
	Fowler	KW	F/S	
	Arnold	GE	F/Lt	
30.12.44	Fitzgerald	P	F/O	Halfiax III
	Stephens	JS	F/S	MZ 801 "T"
	Bicknell	KJA	F/S	Landed at Carnaby
	Parsons	EJ	F/S	due to lack of brake pressure
	Overett	AC	Sgt	
	Pickering	JM	Sgt	
	Meekinson	P	Sgt	

78 Squadron

Date	Name	Initials	Rank	Notes
16.11.44	Wenzel (RCAF)	C	F/O	
	Dixonet	B	Sgt	
	Young (RCAF)	T	F/O	
	Greenslade	J	Sgt	
	Sonoski (RCAF)	F	Sgt	
	Bell	E	Sgt	
	McManus	J	Sgt	

100 Squadron

Date	Name	Initials	Rank	Notes
14.10.44	McVerry (NZ)	RJ	F/O	
	Fallon	J	Sgt	
	Thorby	WJ	F/O	
	Denton	JH	Sgt	
	Carroll (Aus)	JM	F/O	
	Myatt	P	Sgt	
	McNamara	A	Sgt	
28.10.44	Hassler	H	F/O	
	Dorman	WF	P/O	
	Craig (Aus)	HW	F/O	
	Challis	JH	Sgt	
	Christopher	H	Sgt	
	Mills	A	Sgt	
	Nathan	D	Sgt	
28.10.44	Smith	COP	F/O	
	Kieran	J	Sgt	
	Dean (Can)	FG	Sgt	
	Nowlan (Can)	J	Sgt	
	Jones (Can)	CM	Sgt	
	Booth (Can)	GH	Sgt	
	Jenkins (Can)	AWJ	Sgt	
13.04.45	Tarry	PS	W/O	

102 Squadron

Date	Name	Initials	Rank	Notes
08.06.44	Donald (AUS)	HW	P/O	Halifax III
	Brand (AUS)	N	F/S	MZ 298 "F"
	Lathlean (AUS)	RT	F/S	landed at Carnaby
	Skeats	RD	Sgt	
	Rogers (AUS)	DA	F/S	
	Selith	RE	F/S	
	Cook	WJ	Sgt	
08.06.44	Mulvaney (AUS)	GJ	P/O	Halifax III
	Miller	JA	Sgt	MZ 652 "S"
	Duell (AUS)	JB	F/S	landed at Carnaby
	Whellum (AUS)	LK	F/S	
	Heath (AUS)	GS	F/O	
	Bastick (AUS)	TW	Sgt	
	Smith	DG	Sgt	
08.06.44	Sambell (Aus)	SW	P/O	Halifax III
	Curphy	AL	Sgt	MZ 659 "T"
	Beecroft (Aus)	JM	F/S	Crew baled out
	Kidds	CH	Sgt	successfully due to
	Aylmer	AA	Sgt	shortage of petrol
	Magill	SM	Sgt	bad weather conditions
	Criag	JM	Sgt	
08.06.44	Bailey	O	Sgt	Halifax III
	King (CAN)	DG	F/O	MZ 646 "W"
	Bruton	R	F/O	landed at Carnaby
	Newham	AE	P/O	
	Taggart	V	Sgt	
	Cunningham	D	Sgt	
	Jackson	P	Sgt	
08.06.44	Hazelhurst	RAV	F/L	Halifax III
	Dickinson	JE	W/O	LW 160 "A"
	Brainam	EL	Sgt	on mine laying operation
	Warhurst	S	F/S	landed at Carnaby
	Bainbridge	WC	Sgt	
	Appleyard	KGE	Sgt	
	Saunders	FDE	Sgt	

Date	Name	Initials	Rank	Notes
08.06.44	Cooper	DC	P/O	Halifax III
	Twinn	DT	Sgt	MZ 289 "J"
	Foster	HR	Sgt	mine laying
	Lloyd	WF	P/O	landed at Carnaby
	Morris	CM	F/S	
	Draycott	K	Sgt	
	Rowley	C	Sgt	
25.06.44	Hogg (NZ)	RE	P/O	Halifax III
	Thompson (NZ)	A	F/S	LW 179 "E"
	Coldicott	JE	Sgt	landed at Carnaby
	Smith (AUS)	VM	F/S	
	Barnet	L	Sgt	
	Evans	TE	Sgt	
	Pritchard	WE	Sgt	
06.07.44	Budden	PA	F/O	Halifax III
	Stephenson	JA	Sgt	NA 559 "S"
	Ryder	CD	F/O	landed at Carnaby
	Macey	ND	Sgt	
	Creaney	EC	P/O	
	Dooley	S	Sgt	
	Jones	KB	Sgt	
18.08.44	Houghton (AUS)	R	F/S	Halifax III
	Parker	E	Sgt	LW 191 "G"
	Gurnett	E	Sgt	Landed at Carnaby
	Gallagher (AUS)	H	F/S	Port outer engine u/s
	Elliott	PL	Sgt	
	Graham	DE	Sgt	
	Esatoe	R	Sgt	
18.11.44	Meyer	P	Lt	Halifax III
	Rodgers	JH	F/O	LW 168 "C"
	Berger	CR	F/S	Port outer engine u/s
	Roach (NZ)	LM	W/O	
	Allen	DN	Sgt	
	Adlard	HM	Sgt	
	Young	SPA	Sgt	

Date	Name	Initials	Rank	Notes
12.12.44	Hurlburt (CAN)	LH	F/O	Halifax III
	Goodwin (CAN)	G	F/S	LL 581 "W"
	Boyle (CAN)	MJ	F/S	Flaps u/s
	Clayton (CAN)	HJ	W/O	
	Brown (CAN)	WA	Sgt	
	Gemmell (CAN)	CM	F/S	
	Lewis	JB	F/S	
	James	EB	Sgt	
18.12.44	Withington	JG	F/O	Halifax III
	Lyon	JG	F/O	PN 176 E
	Gledhill	F	F/O	No Brake Pressure
	Davies	FL	Sgt	
	Florence	WD	Sgt	
	Fargher	JA	Sgt	
	Williams	R	Sgt	
18.12.44	Smallwoods	RW	F/O	Halifax III
	Russell	W	F/O	LW 142 "N"
	James	BR	F/O	No Brake Pressure
	Hewitt	PDD	Sgt	
	Starmer	NT	F/S	
	Scott	WB	Sgt	
	Gallagher	J	Sgt	
21.12.44	Barr	MK	Sgt	Halifax III
	Hickey	FS	Sgt	NR 186 "U"
	Miller	P	Sgt	Diverted to Carnaby
	Gomm	R	Sgt	
	Smith	JE	Sgt	
	Smith	JE	Sgt	
	Dick	H	Sgt	
21.12.44	Fogg	EW	W/O	Halifax III
	Williams (AUS)	R	W/O	MZ 694 "V"
	Mathews	R	F/S	Diverted to Carnaby
	Fry	CH	F/S	
	Allen	RA	Sgt	
	Hewitson	JD	Sgt	
	Mears	LM	F/S	
	Armstrong	SP	Sgt	

Date	Name	Initials	Rank	Notes
21.12.44	Hurlburt (CAN)	LH	F/O	Halifax III
	Goodwin (CAN)	G	F/S	LL 581 "W"
	Boyle (CAN)	MJ	F/S	Diverted to Carnaby
	Clayton (CAN)	HJ	W/O	
	Brown (CAN)	WA	Sgt	
	Kennady	J	F/S	
	Gemmell (CAN)	CM	F/S	
	James	EB	Sgt	
21.12.44	Helden (SAAF)	RWF	Capt	Halifax III
	Quill (AUS)	W	F/S	LL 597 "Y"
	Boorman	EM	Sgt	Diverted to Carnaby
	Valery (AUS)	JF	F/S	
	Jones	RO	Sgt	
	Johns	RT	Sgt	
	Shrimpton	GW	P/O	
	Morgan	P	F/O	
21.12.44	Lightbody	EH	F/O	Halifax III
	Athurson	A	F/O	NR 242 "E"
	Bolton	AJ	F/S	Diverted to Carnaby
	Peeler (AUS)	ID	F/O	
	Lewis	C	F/S	
	Granville (AUS)	WG	F/S	
	Campbell	EF	Sgt	
21.12.44	Adams	AF	F/O	Halifax III
	Patch	PH	F/S	MZ 830 "C"
	Heery (AUS)	TE	F/O	Diverted to Carnaby
	Hadley	TF	W/O	
	Graham	T	F/S	
	Bryant	WC	F/S	
	Latham	T	P/O	
21.12.44	White	DA	F/L	Halifax III
	Mason	CL	P/O	MZ 827 "K"
	Carsley	CW	F/O	Diverted to Carnaby
	Parrish	EC	P/O	
	Hood	H	Sgt	
	Hiorns	J	Sgt	
	Swainson-Strangeways	RRJ	Sgt	

Date	Name	Initials	Rank	Notes
24.12.44	Russell	WH	F/L	Halifax III
	Forrester	GJ	F/O	MZ 300 "A"
	Sharpe	JD	F/O	Diverted to Carnaby
	Smith	V	F/S	
	Moralee	RS	Sgt	
	Magee	F	Sgt	
	Murphy	DF	Sgt	
24.12.44	Withington	JG	F/O	Halifax III
	Lyon	JG	F/O	NR 242 "B"
	Gledhill	F	F/O	Diverted to Carnaby
	Davies	FL	Sgt	
	Florence	WD	Sgt	
	Fargher	JA	Sgt	
	Williams	R	Sgt	
24.12.44	Rea (SAAF)	WJ	Capt	Halifax III
	McFarlane	DM	Sgt	MZ 426 "D"
	Hewitt	KC	Sgt	Diverted to Carnaby
	Haddock	FA	Sgt	
	Yates	GL	Sgt	
	Seaton	KW	Sgt	
	Hill	J	Sgt	
24.12.44	Gillett (SAAF)	A	Cpt	Halifax III
	Kellagher (AUS)	WR	W/O	NR 225 "E"
	Pike	AG	F/S	Diverted to Carnaby
	Mulaghy (AUS)	RK	F/S	
	Phillips	DR	Sgt	
	Wilson	JH	Sgt	
	Hayes	MR	Sgt	
24.12.44	Meyer	P	Lt	Halifax III
	Rodgers	JH	F/O	MZ 771 "F"
	Berger	CR	F/S	Diverted to Carnaby
	Roach (NZ)	LM	W/O	
	Allen	RA	Sgt	
	Adlard	DM	Sgt	
	Young	SPA	Sgt	

Date	Name	Initials	Rank	Notes
24.12.44	Houghton (AUS)	R	F/S	Halifax III
	Parker	E	Sgt	MZ 79 "H"
	Gurnett	E	Sgt	Diverted to Carnaby
	Gallagher (AUS)	H	F/S	
	Elliott	PL	Sgt	
	Graham	DE	Sgt	
	Esatoe	R	Sgt	
24.12.44	Watson (SAAF)	TF	Cpt	Halifax III
	Nobel (NZ)	LM	F/O	NA 173 "J"
	Murrell (NZ)	RE	F/O	Landed at Carnaby
	Walker (AUS)	SG	F/S	Damaged by flak
	Lewis	HG	Sgt	
	Williams	EB	Sgt	
	Wates (CAN)	RH	Sgt	
24.12.44	Langham (AUS)	M	P/O	Halifax III
	Knight	K	Sgt	MZ 827 "K"
	Sheridan	J	Sgt	Diverted to Carnaby
	Coleman	J	Sgt	
	Westwood	F	Sgt	
	Bettney	S	Sgt	
	Davies	R	Sgt	
24.12.44	Crompton	A	F/O	Halifax III
	Shearon (CAN)	JAG	W/O	MZ 937 "L"
	Thursby	GA	F/O	Diverted to Carnaby
	Harris	AG	F/O	
	Cocks	J	F/O	
	Andrew	J	F/O	
	Robson	RW	Sgt	
24.12.44	Smallwoods	RW	F/O	Halifax III
	Russell	W	F/O	MZ 797 "M"
	James	BR	F/O	Diverted to Carnaby
	Hewitt	PDD	Sgt	
	Starmer	NT	F/S	
	Scott	WB	Sgt	
	Gallagher	J	Sgt	

Date	Name	Initials	Rank	Notes
24.12.44	Cunliffe (AUS)	EA	F/O	Halifax III
	Pickett	EC	F/O	LW 142 "N"
	Turpin (CAN)	JA	F/S	Diverted to Carnaby
	Tinker	F	Sgt	
	Barker	JA	Sgt	
	Linnell	RS	Sgt	
	Stevenson		Sgt	
24.12.44	Roberton	AC	F/S	Halifax III
	Finch	KW	Sgt	LW 179 "P"
	Solyts (CAN)	RS	W/O	Diverted to Carnaby
	Aitken	F	F/S	
	Cramp	JH	F/S	
	Knight	JAH	Sgt	
	Dower	JC	Sgt	
24.12.44	Pearson (CAN)	AI	F/O	Halifax III
	Blair	JJ	F/O	MZ 770 "Q"
	Leslie (CAN)	AI	Sgt	Diverted to Carnaby
	Johnson	TW	Sgt	
	Brown	C	Sgt	
	Middleton	JJ	Sgt	
	Wylie	LJ	Sgt	
24.12.44	Fogg	EW	W/O	Halifax III
	Williams (AUS)	R	W/O	NA 559 "S"
	Mathews	R	F/S	Diverted to Carnaby
	Fry	CH	F/S	
	Allen	RA	Sgt	
	Hewitson	JD	Sgt	
	Kennady	JD	F/S	
	Armstrong	SP	Sgt	
24.12.44	Smith	WR	W/O	Halifax III
	McPherson	WL	F/S	NR 186 "U"
	Kingdon	AJ	Sgt	Diverted to Carnaby
	Crisp	GP	F/O	
	Ollerton	W	Sgt	
	Peckham	B	Sgt	
	Grist	JG	Sgt	

Date	Name	Initials	Rank	Notes
24.12.44	Thomas (AUS)	V	F/O	Halifax III
	Turner	S	Sgt	NR 694 "V"
	White (AUS)	JJ	P/O	Diverted to Carnaby
	Pearson (AUS)	RA	F/S	
	Williamson (AUS)	JW	F/S	
	Goldberg	M	Sgt	
	Shiptin	CW	P/O	
	Hughes	SP	Sgt	
24.12.44	Cronshaw	OC	F/O	Halifax III
	Hollingsworth	BA	P/O	NR 211 "X"
	Dixon (CAN)	JA	P/O	Diverted To Carnaby
	MacCauley	AM	Sgt	
	Fraser		Sgt	
	Horner	PD	Sgt	
	Oliver	JA	P/O	
24.12.44	Jarand	AH	S/L	Halifax III
	Galbraith	D	W/O	LL 597 "Y"
	Davies	EL	F/S	Diverted to Carnaby
	Carter	JM	P/O	
	Telfer	C	F/S	
	Wilson	JM	Sgt	
	Tyler	MJE	F/S	
	Pope	EE	Sgt	
24.12.44	McEvoy	WR	F/L	Halifax III
	Jones	ATB	P/O	NA 615 "Z"
	Mactavish	JA	W/O	Diverted to Carnaby
	Oakley	J	F/O	
	Fleetwood	J	Sgt	
	Tons	RG	P/O	
	Mears	LM	F/S	
	Hickson	TM	P/O	
26.12.44	Lightbody	FBH	F/O	Halifax III
	Athurson	A	F/O	MZ937 "L"
	Duthie	D	W/O	Diverted to Carnaby
	Peeler (AUS)	ID	F/O	
	Granville	WG	F/S	
	Banham	WG	W/O	
	Campbell	EF	Sgt	

Date	Name	Initials	Rank	Notes
26.12.44	Revill	VM	F/L	Halifax III
	Holden	A	F/O	MZ 796 "M"
	McKee	DHA	F/O	Diverted to Carnaby
	Raheley	LK	F/O	
	Johnson	SW	Sgt	
	Williams	BW	Sgt	
	Ripley	SA	Sgt	
26.12.44	Crompton	A	F/O	Halifax III
	Shearon (CAN)	JAG	W/O	LW 142 "N"
	Thursby	GA	F/O	Diverted to Carnaby
	Harris	AG	F/O	
	Cocks	J	F/O	
	Armsby	GEC	F/S	
	Robson	RW	Sgt	
26.12.44	Cunliffe (AUS)	EA	F/O	Halifax III
	Pickett	EC	F/O	NR 966 "G"
	Turpin (CAN)	JA	F/S	Diverted to Carnaby
	Tinker	F	Sgt	
	Barker	JA	Sgt	
	Linnell	RS	Sgt	
	Stevenson	H	Sgt	
26.12.44	Hoyland	P	F/O	Halifax III
	Mitchell (AUS)	WH	W/O	LW 158 "P"
	Stead	WR	F/S	Diverted to Carnaby
	Gildea	MR	F/S	
	Careless	MK	Sgt	
	Mills	LM	F/O	
	Whyte	GA	Sgt	

103 Squadron

Date	Name	Initials	Rank	Notes
12.07.44	Durrant (RCAF)	FG	F/O	
	Matte (RCAF)	LE	Sgt	
	Armstrong	DH	F/S	
	Halliday	JT	Sgt	
	Collard	GM	P/O	
	Webster (RAAF)	SG	W/O	
	Greenway	GT	Sgt	

106 Squadron

Date	Name	Initials	Rank	Notes
27.05.44	Monaghan (AUS)	AS	P/O	Lancaster
	Swinley	CF	Sgt	LM 549
	Philpott	HG	F/Sgt	attacked by enemy fighter
	Wand	NCT	Sgt	on return journey
	Poulter	GA	Sgt	made one wheel
	Gay (CAN)	SF	Sgt	landing at Carnaby
	Sheridan	RK	Sgt	

150 Squadron

Date	Name	Initials	Rank	Notes
16.01.45	Whynacht	KA	F/O	Lancaster I
	Piper	RJ	Sgt	PB 746 X
	Vardigans	KA	Sgt	Forced to land
	Holman	NC	F/O	at Carnaby
	Smith	H	Sgt	
	Paterson	AA	Sgt	
	Hutchings	L	Sgt	

Date	Name	Initials	Rank	Notes
16.01.45	Morris	PH	F/O	Lancaster I
	Davies	JC	Sgt	NG295 W
	Kee	KA	F/S	Forced to land
	Gillies	JH	F/S	at Carnaby
	Masters	RL	F/S	
	Bawden	HH	F/S	
	Griffin	JN	F/S	
16.01.45	Whynacht	KA	F/O	Lancaster I
	Piper	RJ	Sgt	PB 746
	Vardigans	KA	Sgt	landed at Carnaby
	Holman	NC	F/O	
	Smith	H	Sgt	
	Paterson	AA	Sgt	
	Hutchings	L	Sgt	
21.02.45	Sheen DSO		G/C	Lancaster I
	John's		F/Lt	NG 268 G
	and crew			Target Duisburg
				Landed at Carnaby
				due to brake pressure failure
09.04.45	Morgan		P/O	Lancaster
	crew not named			U
				Returned to Carnaby
				on two engines

153 Squadron

Date	Name	Initials	Rank	Notes
30.10.44	Williams (NZ)	RH	F/O	Lancaster
	Dickson	J	Sgt	PB343
	Taylor	AH	Sgt	Struck tree on
	Duigman	DH	P/O	approaching to land
	Cameron	CJ	Sgt	at base and was
	Heath	AR	Sgt	diverted to Carnaby
	Carter	JS	Sgt	damage to undercarriage
				and one engine u/s

Date	Name	Initials	Rank	Notes
02.03.45	Lennox	JM	F/L	Lancaster LM752
	Sykes	E	F/S	Damaged by flak
	Evans	JR	P/O	Hydraulics for undercarriage
	Fulleleve	R	F/O	and bomb doors shot away
	Chalmers	JM	F/O	Belly landing at Carnaby
	Watt	D	F/S	crew unhurt
	Page	DA	P/O	
12.03.45	Crane	NJ	F/O	Lancaster PB786
	Morris	RA	Sgt	Badly damaged by flak
	Whitehead	JH	F/S	
	McGregor	ID	F/S	
	Peel	JL	F/S	
	Smith	E	Sgt	
	Passant	FTA	Sgt	

158 Squadron

Date	Name	Initials	Rank	Notes
6.10.44	Parry	TL	S/L	Halifax
	Huband	EG	F/L	"Z2" MZ 928
	Carroll	PAJ	F/S	Landed at Carnaby
	Spivey	M	F/S	with flaps u/s
	Bateman	A	F/S	
	Hibbert	S	Sgt	
	Dacey	G	Sgt	
14.10.44	Checklin	DS	F/L	Halifax
	McDonald (Aus)	AM	P/O	"S" MZ926
	Littler	G	Sgt	Hit by flak
	Greenhalgh	FH	F/O	Propeller and reduction
	Bosworth	CH	Sgt	gear flew off and
	Formstone	RV	Sgt	injured W/Op's foot
	Graham	PL	Sgt	W/OP removed to hospital

Date	Name	Initials	Rank	Notes
05.12.44	Sharp	WR	F/O	Halifax
	Sessions	JWC	F/S	"K" MZ480
	Millar (Aus)	WJ	W/O	Landed at Carnaby
	Casey (Aus)	KT	F/S	Hydrualics u/s
	Towers	G	Sgt	
	McCarten	F	Sgt	
	Fairless	W	Sgt	
24.12.44	Watson	JS	F/L	HalifaxIII
	Kennedy	RE	F/O	"Z" MZ399
	Day	F	F/S	Hit by flak
	Mason (Aus)	JJ	F/S	damage to nose and fuselage
	Errington	R	F/S	Oxygen bottle in F/Engineer's
	Houldsworth	R	F/S	position had burst
	McCutcheon	G	P/O	
24.12.44	Meredith (CAN)	HRH	F/O	Halifax III
	Mason (CAN)	WRM	F/O	"G" MZ403
	Murray (CAN)	AM	F/S	Landed at Carnaby
	Harper (CAN)	HW	W/O	with no brake pressure
	Springham (CAN)	G	F/S	
	Bower (CAN)	AA	F/S	
	Boyden	DAC	Sgt	
26.12.44	Kuperman (CAN)	A	F/O	Halifax
	Samuels (CAN)	FC	F/C	"E" MZ468
	Scott (CAN)	FA	F/S	landed at Carnaby
	O'Brien (CAN)	WG	Sgt	
	MacDougall (CAN)	SH	Sgt	
	Wood (CAN)	GD	Sgt	
	Noad	LA	Sgt	
26.12.44	Stracham (AUS)	WF	F/O	Halifax III
	Keston	FC	Sgt	"K" MZ480
	Wakefield	JR	Sgt	landed at Carnaby
	Richards	EJ	Sgt	with no brake pressure
	Farrish	A	Sgt	
	Tait	A	Sgt	
	Stow	EH	F/O	

Date	Name	Initials	Rank	Notes
22.01.45	Birch (CAN)	JR	F/O	Halifax III
	McCuaig (CAN)	NE	F/O	"Q" MZ759
	Strang (CAN)	GH	F/O	landed at Carnaby
	Howard	EE	Sgt	with ASI u/s
	Workman (CAN)	JA	Sgt	
	Leigh (CAN)	RG	Sgt	
	Reid	WL	Sgt	
14.02.45	Rogers	CA	F/L	Halifax III
	Harris	DJ	F/O	"W" MZ928
	Houldey	RH	F/S	PI engine caught fire
	Middleton	JV	F/S	engine stopped and prop
	Dent	JJE	Sgt	csu came off
	Farrow	EAJ	Sgt	landed at Carnaby with
	Muir	CJW	P/O	no brake pressure
02.03.45	Houston (CAN)	RB	F/L	Halifax III
	Hunter (CAN)	RE	F/O	"V" NR176
	Langley (CAN)	FB	F/S	SI engines failed
	Hayden (CAN)	WV	F/S	landed at Carnaby
	Barager (CAN)	E	F/S	
	Harris (CAN)	NM	F/S	
	Costigan	W	Sgt	
13.03.45	Checklin	DS	F/L	Halifax III
	McDonald (AUS)	AM	F/O	"Q" MZ759
	Littler	G	F/S	landed at Carnaby
	Greenhalgh	EH	F/C	with no brakes
	Bosworth	CH	Sgt	
	Formstrong	RV	Sgt	
	Graham	PL	Sgt	
20.03.45	Kelham	JF	F/L	Halifax III
	Tebbutt	JA	F/S	"E" NA181
	Healey (AUS)	EKB	W/O	landed at Carnaby
	Wilson (AUS)	JS	F/S	with no brakes
	Fowler	RC	Sgt	
	Williams	JE	Sgt	
	Watson	DRE	Sgt	

Date	Name	Initials	Rank	Notes
11.04.45	Walsh (NZ)	WJ	W/O	Halifax III
	Cox	LCE	P/O	"S" PN444
	Broad	RC	Sgt	hit by flak
	Eckhoff	LJ	Sgt	landed at Carnaby
	Nicholls	AS	Sgt	
	Simpson	AS	Sgt	
	Cook	JA	Sgt	

346 (Guyenne) Squadron

Date	Name	Initials	Rank	Notes
12.06.44	Croblan (FFAF)	M	Adj	Halifax V
	Coupeau (FFAF)	M	S/CH	LK 955
	Guiliocheau (FFAF)	L	Lt	Damaged by flak and
	Kipperle (FFAF)	J	S/CH	Attacked by fighter
	Lhomond (FFAF)	G	Sgt	
	Finale (FFAF)	W	S/CH	
	Biaggi (FFAF)	D	S/CH	
28.06.44	Delluc (FFAF)	P	Adj	Halifax III NA554
	Entressangle (FFAF)	K	Adj	Engine u/s and
	Valentin (FFAF)	R	Lt	No brake pressure
	Le Goff (FFAF)	L	S/C	
	Le Guellec (FFAF)	P	Adj	
	Poli (FFAF)	J	S/C	
	Manick (FFAF)	N	Sgt	
	Cronier (FFAF)	J	Lt	
03.09.44	Beraud (FFAF)	J	Lt	Halifax III LW 438
	Imart (FFAF)	P	S/C	Aircraft hit by flak
	Valette (FFAF)	P	Lt	
	Raffin (FFAF)	P	S/Lt	
	Cloarec (FFAF)	J	S/C	
	Bretton (FFAF)	J	Sgt	
	Manfroy (FFAF)	J	Adj	
	Hannedouche (FFAF)	R	Adj	

Date	Name	Initials	Rank	Notes
02.12.44	Delluc (FFAF)	P	Adj	Halifax III NA 166
	Entressangle (FFAF)	K	Adj	Unable to lock under-
	Valentin (FFAF)	R	Lt	carriage,
	Le Goff (FFAF)	L	S/C	landed at Carnaby
	Le Guellac (FFAF)	P	Adj	
	Poli (FFAF)	J	S/C	
	Borghy (FFAF)	M	Sgt	
21.12.44	Champeaux (FFAF)	L	Adj	Halifax III
	Gondolle (FFAF)	G	Adj	NR232
	Barne (FFAF)	A	CMT	landed at Carnaby
	Paye (FFAF)	C	Lt	
	Aguer (FFAF)	H	A/C	
	Cochois (FFAF)	B	Sgt	
	Delaclaviere (FFAF)	R	Sgt	
24.12.44	Goeppert (FFAF)	A	Cap	Halifax III
	Bonhomme (FFAF)	A	A/C	LL 551
	Aubert (FFAF)	E	Lt	Landed at Carnaby
	Tolu (FFAF)	S	S/C	Hit by Flak
	Spraule (FFAF)	A	S/C	
	Leroy (FFAF)	B	Sgt	
	Lafon (FFAF)	J	Sgt	
24.12.44	Puget (FFAF)	R	A/C	Halifax III
	Meric (FFAF)	Y	S/C	NR229
	Plesch (FFAF)	P	Lt	Landed at Carnaby
	Auriol (FFAF)	A	Adj	Hit by Flak
	Jaffeux (FFAF)	P	S/C	
	Borg (FFAF)	G	S/C	
	Senlemes (FFAF)	A	S/C	
24.12.44	Gronier (FFAF)	J	Cap	Halifax III
	Hopp (FFAF)	R	Adj	MZ 709
	Pavoitti (FFAF)	G	Lt	Landed at Carnaby
	Roy (FFAF)	J	Cap	
	Duran (FFAF)	P	S/C	
	Kergrene (FFAF)	L	S/C	
	Isst (FFAF)	A	Adj	

Date	Name	Initials	Rank	Notes
24.12.44	Cronlan (FFAF)	M	Adj	Halifax III
	Monchlet (FFAF)	M	S/C	MZ 477
	Mecak (FFAF)	J	Lt	Landed at Carnaby
	Lasserre (FFAF)	J	Adj	
	W [illegible] (FFAF)	P	Adj	
	Croquot (FFAF)	C	Sgt	
	Rev (FFAF)	M	Sgt	
24.12.44	Gonthier (FFAF)	A	Lt	Halifax III
	Blaise (FFAF)	R	Adj	MZ 738
	Capdeville (FFAF)	P	S/Lt	Landed at Carnaby
	Dussaut (FFAF)	A	Sgt	
	Heynaud (FFAF)	R	Sgt	
	St Gevin (FFAF)	V	Sgt	
	Helmuth (FFAF)	R	Sgt	
24.12.44	Delvoye (FFAF)	C	Lt	Halifax III
	Marranner (FFAF)	M	Sgt	LW 438
	Baldassari (FFAF)	C	Lt	Landed at Carnaby
	Capparos (FFAF)	E	Lt	
	Vigne (FFAF)	W	Sgt	
	Codepert (FFAF)	A	Sgt	
	Graziani (FFAF)	J	Sgt	
24.12.44	Champeaux (FFAF)	L	Adj	Halifax III
	Gondolle (FFAF)	G	Adj	NR232
	Barne (FFAF)	A	CMT	landed at Carnaby
	Paye (FFAF)	C	Lt	hit by flak
	Aguer (FFAF)	H	A/C	
	Cochois (FFAF)	B	Sgt	
	Delaclaviere (FFAF)	R	Sgt	
24.12.44	Vantroyer (FFAF)	A	Adj	Halifax III
	Hielot (FFAF)	H	S/C	NA 556
	Plagnard (FFAF)	G	Cap	Landed at Carnaby
	Noel (FFAF)	G	Lt	
	Hervelin (FFAF)	L	Sgt	
	Iche (FFAF)	A	Sgt	
	Allain (FFAF)	M	Sgt	

Date	Name	Initials	Rank	Notes
24.12.44	Boe (FFAF)	L	Cap	Halifax III
	Caristan (FFAF)	H	Lt	MZ 490
	Demazure (FFAF)	R	CMT	Landed at Carnaby
	Ruellan (FFAF)	Q	Lt	Hit by flak
	Ploye (FFAF)	R	S/C	
	Azema (FFAF)	L	Sgt	
	Bressen (FFAF)	A	Sgt	
24.12.44	Idrac (FFAF)	M	Lt	Halifax III
	Traclet (FFAF)	A	Adj	NA 564
	Immupilliers (FFAF)		CMT	Landed at Carnaby
	Larue (FFAF0	R	S/C	
	Cavoye (FFAF)	J	Sgt	
	Boufpand (FFAF)	J	Sgt	
	Routhier (FFAF)	J	Sgt	
24.12.44	Marchall (FFAF)	F	Cap	Halifax III
	Muliner (FFAF)	G	Sgt	LL 553
	Troiux (FFAF)	C	Lt	Landed at Carnaby
	Munier (FFAF)	M	S/L	
	Rebierre (FFAF)	I	Sgt	
	Padre (FFAF)	P	Sgt	
	Godart (FFAF)	L	S/C	
	Bayle (FFAF)	P	Asp	
24.12.44	Bourgain (FFAF)	L	Cap	Halifax III
	Bourgeois (FFAF)	M	S/C	MZ 741
	Duvert (FFAF)	R	Lt	Landed at Carnaby
	Beauvois (FFAF)	A	Adj	Hit by flak
	Dufour (FFAF)	C	S/C	
	Garrido (FFAF)	C	S/C	
	Ruffie (FFAF)	M	S/C	
24.12.44	Brion (FFAF)	A	Cap	Halifax III
	Richard (FFAF)	R	Adj	MA 737
	Barthelot (FFAF)	J	Lt	Landed at Carnaby
	Demesmay (FFAF)	M	S/Lt	
	Darribehaude (FFAF)		S/C	
	Poures (FFAF)	R	Sgt	
	Connot (FFAF)	R	S/C	

Date	Name	Initials	Rank	Notes
26.12.44	Brion (FFAF)	A	Cap	Halifax III PN 365
	Richard (FFAF)	R	Adj	FIDO assisted landing
	Barthelot (FFAF)	L	Lt	
	Demesmay (FFAF)	M	S/Lt	
	Darribehaude (FFAF)		Sgt	
	Pouress (FFAF)	P	Sgt	
	Connot (FFAF)	R	S/C	
26.12.44	Busnel (FFAF)	R	S/C	Halifax III PN 170
	Chomy (FFAF)	W	A/C	FIDO assisted landing
	Vialette (FFAF)	A	Lt	
	Sutour (FFAF)	M	Lt	
	Bonnapous (FFAF)	P	S/C	
	Helary(FFAF)	J	Sgt	
	Baret (FFAF)	M	Sgt	
26.12.44	Bourgain (FFAF)	L	Cap	Halifax III MZ 486
	Bourgeois (FFAF)	M	S/C	FIDO assisted landing
	Duvert (FFAF)	R	Lt	
	Beauvois (FFAF)	A	Adj	
	Dufour (FFAF)	C	S/C	
	Garrido (FFAF)	C	S/C	
	Ruffie (FFAF)	M	S/C	
26.12.44	Delluc (FFAF)	P	Adj	Halifax III NA 166
	Entressangle (FFAF)	K	Adj	FIDO assisted landing
	Valentin (FFAF)	R	Lt	
	Le Goff (FFAF)	L	S/C	
	Hautin (FFAF)	J	S/C	
	Poli(FFAF)	J	S/C	
	Borghy (FFAF)	M	Sgt	
26.12.44	Boe (FFAF)	L	Cap	Halifax III Nz 488
	Caristan (FFAF)	H	Lt	FIDO assisted landing
	Demazure (FFAF)	R	CMT	
	Ruellan (FFAF)	G	S/Lt	
	Ploye (FFAF)	R	S/C	
	Azema (FFAF)	L	Sgt	
	Kresson (FFAF)	A	Sgt	

Date	Name	Initials	Rank	Notes
22.01.45	Barrat (FFAF)	R	CMT	Halifax III MZ488
	Carayol (FFAF)	G	S/C	landed at Carnaby
	Pluchard (FFAF)	L	CAP	
	Perseval (FFAF)	R	Lt	
	Mourey (FFAF)	M	Sgt	
	Cardiol (FFAF)	H	S/C	
	Potet (FFAF)	C	A/C	
02.03.45	Busnel (FFAF)	R	S/C	Halifax III PN170
	Chomi (FFAF)	W	S/Lt	landed at Carnaby
	Vialatte (FFAF)	A	Lt	
	Sutour (FFAF)	M	Lt	
	Bonnapous (FFAF)	P	S/C	
	Helary (FFAF)	J	Sgt	
	Baret (FFAF)	M	Sgt	
11.04.45	Duvillard (FFAF)	R	Lt	Halifax III MZ 709
	Ingargiola (FFAF)	A	Sgt	Landed at Carnaby
	Grunberg (FFAF)	R	S/Lt	
	Rohrwansser (FFAF)	M	S/C	
	Gioux (FFAF)	R	S/C	
	Boubilat (FFAF)	P	Sgt	
	Clergerie (FFAF)	A	S/C	

347 (Tunisie) Squadron (French)

Date	Name	Initials	Rank	Notes
23.7.44	Berthet (FFAF)	C	Lt	Halifax III
	Paturle (FFAF)	P	Lt	LW642
	Julaire (FFAF)	A	Cpt	
	Madule (FFAF)	J	Adj	
	Jenoer (FFAF)	R	S/C	
	Ocer (FFAF)	R	Adj	
	Eyraud (FFAF)	J	S/C	

Date	Name	Initials	Rank	Notes
08.08.44	Lau (FFAF)		Lt	Halifax III
	Beguet (FFAF)		Sgt	NA 519
	Schelegel (FFAF)		Lt	undercarriage u/s
	Dabiton (FFAF)		S/C	
	Leglaire (FFAF)		Adj	
	Giraudin (FFAF)		Adj	
	Difielig (FFAF)		S/C	
15.08.44				aircraft landed at Carnaby details unknown
11.09.44	Deleuze	A	Lt	Halifax III
	Juste		S/C	LL557
	Courvalin	L	LT	
	Vezoills		ASF	
	Chaboud	F	Sgt	
	Bastlan	L	Sgt	
	Meau	L	Sgt	
05.12.44	Pinaud (FFAF)	H	Lt	Halifax III
	Roy (FFAF)		Adj	LL 556
	Hachette (FFAF)	R	Cap	Loss of brake pressure
	Loridan (FFAF)	M	Lt	Landed at Carnaby
	Lagouttiere (FFAF)		Adj	
	Vigny (FFAF)	H	S/C	
	Buignet (FFAF)	R	S/C	
26.12.44	Caniellikr (FFAF)	M	Lt	Halifax III
	Lefervre (FFAF)	V	S/C	NR 235
	Vauche (FFAF)	A	Capt	
	Pehuet (FFAF)	J	Lt	FIDO assisted Landing
	Clairiesford v	H	Lt	owing to weather
	D'Andera (FFAF)	R	Sgt	
	Pre (FFAF)	J	S/C	
	Dufour D Latthe (FFAF)		CMT	

Date	Name	Initials	Rank	Notes
26.12.44	Aulen (FFAF)	J	A/C	Halifax III
	Patry (FFAF)	R	S/C	NA 182
	Stanilas (FFAF)	G	CAP	FIDO assisted Landing
	Rognant (FFAF)	C	S/Lt	owing to weather
	Berdeaux (FFAF)	H	S/C	
	Bordier (FFAF)	M	Sgt	
	Bordelais (FFAF)	R	Sgt	
26.12.44	Bonnet (FFAF)	R	Cap	Halifax III
	Mauper (FFAF)	H	S/Lt	NA 174
	Allegre (FFAF)	P	Cap	FIDO assisted Landing
	Reou (FFAF)	G	Lt	owing to weather
	Bozec (FFAF)	P	A/C	
	Boyeau (FFAF)	A	Sgt	
	Mand (FFAF)	A	A/C	
01.01.45	Lafaye (FFAF)		Cap	FIDO assisted landing
				L8/O
				Diverted to Carnaby
14.01.45	Petus (FFAF)	C	Lt	Halifax III
	Trimert (FFAF)		Adj	ME 515
	Dressesard (FFAF)	C	Lt	Landed at Carnaby
	Mignon(FFAF)	J	Lt	
	Coquerou (FFAF)	J	S/C	
	Lindenerg (FFAF)	A	Adj	
	Riviere (FFAF)	F	S/C	
17.02.45	Vidal (FFAF)	A	Adc	crash landed at Carnaby
	Portesseau (FFAF)	L	Adj	following fire in outer port
	Guenois (FFAF)	L	Ltn	engine
	Piccot (FFAF)	G	Slt	
	Chanson (FFAF)	J	Sgc	
	Bruno (FFAF)	A	Adj	
	Pizel (FFAF)	R	Sgt	

Date	Name	Initials	Rank	Notes
25.03.45	Coupvent (FFAF)	L	ASP	Halifax III
	Lavocat (FFAF)	F	Sgt	LW678
	Bourgorin (FFAF)	G	R/L	
	Drevet (FFAF)	G	ASP	
	Lenfant (FFAF)	J	S/C	
	Laffont (FFAF)	G	Sgt	
	Dilius (FFAF)	R	Sgt	

405 Squadron

Date	Name	Initials	Rank	Notes
02.6.45	Hartley	JR	F/O	

415 Squadron

Date	Name	Initials	Rank	Notes
15.10.44	Kerr	JL	F/O	Halifax Y
	Ballhartz	HJG	F/S	diverted to Carnaby
	Hayes	RA	P/O	
	Varyard (CAN)	GF	W/O	
	Willson	EJ	F/S	
	James	RL	F/S	
	Atkins (RAF)	D	F/S	
	Glaistor (RAF)	LP	F/S	
06.12.44	Northrup	JR	F/L	Halifax
	Thauvotte	RB	F/O	MZ 947 "K"
	Paradis	JP	F/S	Landed at Carnaby
	D'Amboies	JC	P/O	due to lack of brake
	Sullivan	JA	F/S	pressure
	Lochaneo	JC	Sgt	
	Bryden	AL	Sgt	
	Roy	CA	F/S	

Date	Name	Initials	Rank	Notes
14.02.45	McKenzie	JS	P/O	Halifax III
	Herring	RK	F/S	NA 185 "B"
	Fuller	LA	F/O	landed at Carnaby
	Bailey	SA	F/S	due to hydraulics u/s
	Palmer	EP	P/O	
	Duffy	OG	P/O	
	Charloboie	DL	F/S	
25.03.45	Clark	VG	W/O	Halifax
	Kirk	WH	F/O	ME 239 "V"
	Page	AS	F/S	
	Delanger	JR	F/S	
	Fortin	NJ	F/S	
	Catos	GD	F/O	
	Minnikin	K	Sgt	
25.03.45	Details unknown			Halifax
				"B"
				Landed at Carnaby

419 Squadron

Date	Name	Initials	Rank	Notes
20.09.44	McDonald	LH	WO2	Lancaster X
	Reid	DL	F/S	KB 797
	Ritchie	W	F/S	K
	Johnson	FC	F/S	Target Calais
	Greenwood	J	Sgt	Landed at Carnaby
	Wilson	WH		
	Shettler		F/S	

420 Squadron

Date	Name	Initials	Rank	Notes
16.08.44	Kidd	KR	P/O	Halifax III
	Lafranier	VG	F/O	LL589 "N"
	Battrick	WT	WO2	on returning another aircraft
	Thomson	IJ	Sgt	cut across pilot's canopy.
	Lowe	S	F/S	Damage to both port props and
	Paterson	EW	F/S	starboard prop, Tailplate hole.
	Inglis	DJ	Sgt	Landed at Carnaby
	Decary	J	F/S	Accident at 01.41 hrs
28.09.44	Jones	GJL	F/L	Halifax III
	Robinson	RA	F/O	MZ952 "I"
	Penlum	RJ	F/O	Landed at Carnaby
	Reid	R	WO1	without brake pressure
	Heaton	GA	F/S	
	Stewart	RC	F/S	
	Lauder (RAF)	J	Sgt	
23.10.44	Austenson	OH	F/O	Halifax III
	Jamieson	GK	F/O	LW 388 "G"
	West	FJ	Sgt	Damage to bomb doors
	Coleman	HG	P/O	Aircraft landed at Carnaby
	Evens	RG	F/S	no brake pressure
	Lyon	JR	F/S	
	Mosses	JE	Sgt	
30.10.44	McCutcheson	EB	F/O	Halifax III
	Welk	JG	F/O	NR 138 "T"
	Ritchie	DW	F/O	Bomb door carried away
	Fuller	FM	P/O	at time of jettisoning
	Haacke	GA	F/S	Landed at Carnaby
	Mackey	DO	Sgt	
	Wylie	BA	Sgt	
16.01.45	Field	RBT	F/O	Halifax
				Landed at Carnaby due to
				collision with another aircraft
06.03.45	Tederan (RCAF)	M	F/O	

Date	Name	Initials	Rank	Notes
25.03.45	Simonson	LC	F/O	Halifax III
	Stephen	AM	P/O	NR139 "A"
	Russell	RF	F/O	Hit by flak
	Rogers	DW	WO2	Hole in port tank and
	Hawke	WH	WO2	port inner cowling and
	Lussier	KE	F/O	rear turret
	McLaren	GM	Sgt	Landed at Carnaby
25.03.45	Lepp	RJ	F/O	Halifax III
	Angelson	JR	F/O	LV953 "F"
	Brownell	RC	F/O	Landed at Carnaby
	Draper	ID	F/S	
	Cormack	GR	F/S	
	Arsenault	JW	F/S	
	Bartlett	WJ	Sgt	

424 Squadron

Date	Name	Initials	Rank	Notes
09.08.44	Kendrick	PG	F/O	Halifax III "Q" LW117
	Southman	FG	F/O	Landed at Carnaby
	Cooper	AJ	Sgt	No Brake Pressure
	Anchintz	JR	P/O	Bombing Prodville
	Bart	RW	Sgt	
	[illegible]	HD	Sgt	
	Wilson	RE	Sgt	J167008
18.08.44	Chance	DG	P/O	Halifax III
	Hanson	EL	F/O	"J" LW132
	Collis	WD	F/O	Bombing Connantre
	McLean	LO	Sgt	Landed at Carnaby
	Cardall	L	Sgt	throttle problem with
	Griffith	CB	Sgt	starboard outer engine
	Dufresne	LA	Sgt	

115

Date	Name	Initials	Rank	Notes
14.10.44	Chance	DG	P/O	Halifax
	Hanson	EL	F/O	"J" LW 131
	Collis	WD	F/O	Loss of brake pressure
	McLean	LO	Sgt	Diverted to Carnaby
	Cardall	L	Sgt	
	Griffith	CB	Sgt	
	Dufresne	LA	Sgt	
06.11.44	Lefebvre	ER	F/O	Halifax III
	Pappas	SG	F/O	"C" LW 131
	Kutch	P	F/O	Bombing Gelsenkerchen
	Norton	ER	F/O	Port outer and starboard
	Tweed	LO	Sgt	engine u/s
	Carr	HD	Sgt	Landed at Carnaby
	Hyde	LH	Sgt	

425 Squadron

Date	Name	Initials	Rank	Notes
30.10.44	Sequin & crew		F/O	Halifax III LL596 "U" Landed at Carnaby
30.10.44	Mark & crew		F/O	Halifax III NR 178 "J" Landed at Carnaby
01.11.44	Smith		F/O	Halifax MZ 831 "Z" Landed at Carnaby due to low brake pressure
21.11.44	Gordeau & crew		F/L	Halifax III MZ 714 "Y" Diverted to Carnaby

426 Squadron

Date	Name	Initials	Rank	Notes
06.10.44	Lowe	JW	F/L	Halifax MkVII
	Cutt	KE	F/O	LW 203 "F"
	Daneberger	JT	Sgt	
	Leggat	WJ	F/S	
	Johnson (RAF)	PT	F/S	
	Dane	FG	WO1	
	Nelson	RC	F/S	
14.10.44	McKay	AH	P/O	Halifax MkVII
	McQuade	JS	F/O	LN 199 "C"
	Schmu?	BH	WO2	Landed at Carnaby
	Garries	IR	F/O	due to lack of fuel
	Welton (RAF)	RJ	Sgt	
	Scherling	RH	F/S	
	Tinling	PT	F/S	

429 Squadron

Date	Name	Initials	Rank	Notes
14.10.44	Drewery (CAN)	BE	P/O	Halifax III
	Catheralle (CAN)	LJG	F/O	"O" MZ288
	Cullen (CAN)	LFJ	F/O	Bombing Duisburg
	Richmond (RAF)	JD	Sgt	Hydraulics u/s
	McDonald (CAN)	AR	F/S	Diverted to Carnaby
	Kelly (CAN)	KE	Sgt	
	Giblin (CAN)	JR	Sgt	
28.10.44	Drewery (CAN)	BE	P/O	Halifax III
	Catheralle (CAN)	LJG	F/O	"O" MZ288
	Cullen (CAN)	LFJ	F/O	Bombing Cologne
	Richmond (RAF)	JD	Sgt	Landed at Carnaby
	McDonald (CAN)	AR	F/S	Due to shortage of petrol
	Kelly (CAN)	KE	Sgt	
	Giblin (CAN)	JR	Sgt	

Date	Name	Initials	Rank	Notes
28.10.44	Hay (CAN)	G	P/O	Halifax III
	Savard (CAN)	RL	F/O	"T" LW964
	Tremblay (CAN)	JJM	F/S	Bombing Cologne
	Nicholson (RAF)	FJ	Sgt	Landed at Carnaby
	Couzens (RAF)	RH	P/O	Due to shortage of petrol
	Brown (CAN)	FN	F/S	
	Gabrial (CAN)	TA	F/S	
28.10.44	MacDonald (CAN)	AM	F/O	Halifax III
	Codd (CAN)	P	F/O	"F" MZ318
	Pegg (CAN)	HC	F/O	Bombing Cologne
	Wood (RAF)	TM	Sgt	Landed at Carnaby
	Urquhart (CAN)	RT	F/S	for refuelling
	McDougall (CAN)	JB	Sgt	
	Mason (CAN)	KM	Sgt	
29.10.44	Humphries (CAN) and crew	HAM	F/O	Halifax III "T" LW964 Bombing Oberlar Landed at Carnaby due to lack of brake pressure
30.12.44	Moffatt (CAN) and crew	LC	F/O	Halifax III "R" MZ303 Landed at Carnaby due to brake failure Bombing Cologne/Kalk Nord

431 Squadron

Date	Name	Initials	Rank	Notes
01.12.44	Harrison	RW	F/L	

Date	Name	Initials	Rank	Notes
03.08.44	Notley (Aus)	LJ	P/O	ND 822
	Caley	SJ	Sgt	Hit by heavy flak
	Milligan	E	P/O	Leading edge of
	Pender	W	Sgt	starboard wing holed.
	Greene	JP	Sgt	Bomb doors failed to open,
	Goldstone	DA	F/S	landed with full bomb load.
	Owen	JH	Sgt	
29.08.44	Hudson (AUS)	NH	F/O	ND 967
	Thatcher	JV	Sgt	Collided with another aircraft
	Lucas (AUS)	VH	W/O	25 miles short of target
	Jackson (AUS)	GN	W/O	Extensive damage
	McIntosh	CA	F/S	"scraped along to Carnaby"
	Parr	AA	F/S	
	Frail (AUS)	AE	F/S	
14.08.45	Eaton (Aus)	BJ	F/O	Lancaster PB 352
	Malin	R	Sgt	Petrol Leak
	Long	NJ	Sgt	Diverted to Carnaby
	Pyvie	R	F/O	
	MacDonald (Aus)	DH	F/S	
	Greenhalgh?	DH	Sgt	
	Cavanagh	T	Sgt	
14.08.45	Marshall (Aus)	ED	F/O	Lancaster PB816
	Chapman	PR	Sgt	Sickness of member
	Williams	SL	Sgt	of crew
	Phillips	D	Sgt	Diverted to Carnaby
	Sillock (Aus)	KM	F/S	
	Nell	E	Sgt	
	Croft	JDR	Sgt	

462 Squadron

Date	Name	Initials	Rank	Notes
27.08.44	Cuttriss (Aus)	AG	P/O	Halifax III
	Gibson (Aus)	JR	F/S	LV 955
	Clarke (Aus)	KT	F/S	Crippled bomber
	Trowbridge (Aus)	JD	F/S	emergency landing
	Rahalay (Aus)	LK	F/S	at Carnaby
	Dyer (Aus)	WE	Sgt	
	Hall	DC	Sgt	
03.09.44	Mitchell (Aus)	TR	F/Sgt	Halifax III
	Latimer	JF	F/Sgt	LL600
	McCorkindale	W	Sgt	Driffield closed due
	Scott (Aus)	RW	F/Sgt	to bad weather
	Thornton (Aus)	AM	F/Sgt	
	Maguire(Aus)	TL	F/Sgt	
	Kellard	S	Sgt	
06.10.44	James (Aus)	MH	F/O	Halifax III
	Toede (Aus)	NH	F/S	NR119
	MacFarlane (Aus)	TH	W/C	
	Fraser (Aus)	JD	F/S	
	Calman (Aus)	HW	F/S	
	Ladwith (Aus)	TF	F/S	
	Botham	SC	Sgt	
06.10.44	Taylor (Aus)	BM	W/C	Halifax III
	Lobb (Aus)	AC	F/S	NP989
	Smith (Aus)	NA	Sgt	
	Weston (Aus)	FW	F/S	
	Somerville	DF	Sgt	
	Dyer	GH	Sgt	
	Manning	WA	Sgt	
04.11.44	Marchant (Aus)	RE	P/O	Halifax III
	Tattersall (Aus)	KG	F/S	LK 460
	O'Donoghue (Aus)	JN	F/S	
	Blundell (Aus)	R	F/S	
	Mannell (Aus)	LG	F/S	
	Sharpe (Aus)	RR	F/O	
	Brocklesby	LG	Sgt	

Date	Name	Initials	Rank	Notes
04.11.44	Byrom (Aus)	JE	P/O	Halifax III
	Simms (Aus)	BA	F/S	NA 621
	Maxwell	WW	SGt	
	Kelly (Aus)	PA	F/S	
	Simms (Aus)	OE	F/S	
	Kavanagh	MJ	Sgt	
	Hartop	NA	Sgt	
	Morton	JL	Sgt	
21.11.44	Sharp	GC	F/S	Halifax
	Payne	HK	F/S	LV955
	Bland	GS	F/S	
	Peachey (Aus)	KC	F/S	
	Powell	KE	Sgt	
	Mackie	J	Sgt	
	Helden	C	Sgt	
21.11.44	Lodder (Aus)	AM	P/O	Halifax
	Naylor	AM	Sgt	MZ306
	Windus	E	Sgt	
	Foster (Aus)	CRH	F/S	
	Casterton	RE		
	McGarvie	R	Sgt	
	Hollins	J	Sgt	
21.11.44	Boyd	JN	P/O	Halifax III
	Hamilton	KE		NA619
	Mortimer	J		
	Evans	W		
	Compton	B		
	Spriggs	K		
	Taylor	FO		
22.11.44	Ely (Aus)	WC	F/O	Halifax III
	Millhouse	B	F/O	MZ398
	Critchley	DJ	Sgt	
	Herring (Aus)	PH	F/O	
	Robinson	T	Sgt	
	Ogilvie	N	Sgt	
	Hetherington	R	Sgt	

Date	Name	Initials	Rank	Notes
01.02.45	Britt (Aus)	L	F/O	Halifax III
	Creswick (Aus)	AH	W/O	MZ37 Z5-L
	Cruickshank (Aus)	HJ	F/S	Landed at Carnaby
	Chaplin (Aus)	JP	F/S	due to defective brakes
	Spillane (Aus)	JT	F/S	
	Kerkell (Aus)	RJ	F/S	
	Bunting	ET	Sgt	
	Tisdell (Aus)	ED	F/S	

463 Squadron

Date	Name	Initials	Rank	Notes
09.02.45	Wickes (RAAF)	MS	F/O	On ops to Politz ED 611
	Botting	LR	Sgt	attacked by 2 night fighters, PI
	Brownlee (RAAF)	RS	F/O	engine u/s
	Brett (RAAF)	FK	W/O	
	Jenkins (RAAF)	RJ	F/S	
	Boddy	FH	Sgt	
	Cottroll	LD	Sgt	

466 Squadron

Date	Name	Initials	Rank	Notes
12.07.44	Cuttriss (Aus)	AG	P/O	Halifax III
	Gibson (Aus)	JR	F/S	ME294
	Clarke (Aus)	KT	F/S	
	Trowbridge (Aus)	JD	F/S	
	Rahalay (Aus)	LK	F/S	
	Dyer (Aus)	WE	Sgt	
	Hall	DC	Sgt	

Date	Name	Initials	Rank	Notes
20.07.44	Kagleton (Aus)	WE	F/L	Halifax III
	Cornwell (Aus)	HC	F/O	LW172
	Wade (Aus)	JE	F/O	
	Hayes	RC	F/O	
	McCosker (Aus)	BW	P/O	
	Brown	J	F/S	
	Green	WC	Sgt	
01.08.44	Plasto (Aus)	LJ	P/O	Halifax III LW857
	Todd (Aus)	JC	P/O	Bomb attack on Chappelle
	Moran (Aus)	JH	P/O	Notre Dame
	Russell	CA	Sgt	Diverted to Carnaby poor
	Tyers (Aus)	RC	F/S	weather conditions
	Devereux	CJ	F/S	
	Morley	AE	Sgt	
01.08.44	Kenyon (Aus)	T	P/O	Halifax III LN904
	White Aus)	B	Sgt	Bomb attack on Chappelle
	Klezel Aus)	RC	F/S	Notre Dame
	McManus (Aus)	TA	F/S	Diverted to Carnaby poor
	Robinson (Aus)	NF	F/S	weather conditions
	Herne (Aus)	FM	F/S	
	Jack	PD	Sgt	
01.08.44	Burrow (Aus)	LF	F/S	Halifax III LW172
	Surgeoner (Aus)	G	F/S	Bomb attack on Chappelle
	Johnston (Aus)	MM	F/S	Notre Dame
	Goodsell (Aus)	HR	F/S	Diverted to Carnaby poor
	Lusted (Aus)	RB	F/S	weather conditions
	Lusk (Aus)	FS	F/S	
	Mackay	PG	Sgt	
01.08.44	Herman (Aus)	JB	P/O	Halifax III
	Underwood (Aus)	D	F/S	Bomb attack on Chappelle
	Nicholson (Aus)	W	F/O	Notre Dame
	Duncan (Aus)	A	F/S	Diverted to Carnaby poor
	Wilson (Aus)	MM	F/S	weather conditions
	Vivash (Aus)	JM	F/S	

Date	Name	Initials	Rank	Notes
18.08.44	MacDermott (Aus)	BJ	S/L	Halifax III MZ 792
	Hines (Aus)	WA	P/O	Hydraulics U/S
	Saunders	LT	P/O	Bomb doors would not close
	Evans	T	F/S	
	Dodd	WV	F/S	
	Shoemaker	WS	P/O	
	Brown	N McA	Sgt	
27.08.44	Plasto (Aus)	LJ	P/O	Halifax III LW 837
	McNulty (Aus)	PJ	P/O	Bomb attack on Homberg
	Todd (Aus)	JC	P/O	
	Moran (Aus)	JH	P/O	
	Russell	CA	Sgt	
	Tyers (Aus)	RC	F/S	
	Devereux	CJ	F/S	
	Morley	AE	Sgt	
10.09.44	Herman (RAAF)	JB	F/L	Landed at Carnaby - reason
	Underwood (RAAF)	D	F/S	unknown
	Nicholson (RAAF)	W	F/O	On bombing attack to Le Havre.
	Duncan (RAAF)	A	F/S	
	Wilson (RAAF)	MN	F/S	
	Vivash	JM	F/S	
	Knotts	HW	Sgt	
02.11.44	Dodgson (Aus)	NOR	P/O	Halifax 111
	Tolhurst (Aus)	HJ	F/S	NR168
	Ryder (Aus)	EM	F/S	
	McCasker (Aus)	EA	W/O	
	Stopher (Aus)	RD	W/O	
	McLay (Aus)	JS	F/S	
	Caffrey	F	Sgt	

467 Squadron

Date	Name	Initials	Rank	Notes
28.10.44	Boxsell DFC (RAAF)	WK	F/O	On ops to Bergen LM746 was
	Bauchop	RJ	Sgt	involved in a collision near
	Aubourg (RAAF)	VE	F/Sgt	Mablethorpe
	Pegler	L	F/Sgt	4 of the crew bailed out and pilot
	Leach (RAAF)	HH	F/Sgt	F/E and navigator stayed on and
	Stokes (RAAF)	JR	F/Sgt	landed at Carnaby
	Leonard (RAAF)	NCK	F/Sgt	

578 Squadron

Date	Name	Initials	Rank	Notes
27.05.44	Bluring	J	Sgt	Halifax III
	McNaughton (CAN))	AE	F/O	LW 496
	Majaki	BA	Sgt	LK "O"
	Costidell	GA	Sgt	Attacked and damaged by
	Sheasby	KC	Sgt	Dornier 217
	Romback	PB	Sgt	W/OP injured
	Adams	CW	Sgt	Landed at Carnaby
08.06.44	Henderson	GN	F/O	Halifax III
	Smith	PJ	Sgt	MZ559
	MacDonald	WW	F/S	LK "P"
	Whitewell	NS	Sgt	Landed at Carnaby
	Trousdale	M	Sgt	
	Wilkinson	WJ	Sgt	
	Grey	PJ	F/O	
08.06.44	Fox	EW	F/S	Halifax III
	Goldsmid	P	F/S	LK846
	Howatson	GJ	F/S	LK "R"
	Middleton	FW	Sgt	Landed at Carnaby
	Hodgson	G	Sgt	
	Johnson (AUS)	DJ	Sgt	
	Dey	LN	Sgt	

Date	Name	Initials	Rank	Notes
28.06.44	Bleakley (CAN)	RM	F/L	Halifax III
	Pringle (CAN)	JA	F/O	MZ 583
	Johnson (CAN)	WA	F/O	LK "Y"
	Jackson	K	F/O	Damaged by flak
	Roberts	JA	Sgt	Bomb-aimer injured
	Ward	GD	Sgt	Landed at Carnaby
	Dickenson	A	Sgt	
06.07.44	Williams	WJ	F/L	Halifax III
	Grantham	GL	F/O	LN 543
	Degryse (CAN)	JC	F/S	LK "E"
	Grogan	JC	Sgt	
	Blackmore	FC	Sgt	
	Brice	F	F/S	
	Polmer	R	Sgt	
20/21.07.44	Clark	MH	F/O	Halifax III
	Binns (CAN)	JRS	F/O	LW 346
	Williams (CAN)	LE	F/O	LK"Z"
	Young	RC	F/S	Landed at Carnaby
	Richards	WG	Sgt	
	Scorer	JRS	Sgt	
	Roberts	L	F/S	
16/17.08.44	Horton (CAN)	EL	F/S	Halifax III
	Smith	RS	Sgt	NA 605
	Grime (CAN)	FG	F/S	LK "R"
	Andrean	R	Sgt	No brake pressure
	Olleranshaw	JE	Sgt	Landed at Carnaby
	Casserly	W	Sgt	
	Gedrim	JO	Sgt	
03.09.44	Allen	JH	F/O	Halifax III
	Dudley	CJ	P/O	LW 47.
	Phillips	NM	F/S	LK "B"
	Adams	RE	F/S	Landed at Carnaby
	Stobbs	R	Sgt	
	Wilkinson	WJ	F/S	
	Dunton	EG	Sgt	

Date	Name	Initials	Rank	Notes
03.09.44	Archer	J	F/L	Halifax III
	Wainwright	HE	F/S	NA 574
	Tempest	JL	F/L	LK "D"
	Armstrong	W	W/O	Landed at Carnaby
	Bound	R	W/O	
	Tucker	HS	W/O	
	Eaton	H	Sgt	
03.09.44	Sanders	GE	F/S	Halifax III
	Munn (CAN)	J	F/O	LK 809
	Elliott	RN	F/O	LK "H"
	Quaggin	JD	F/S	Landed at Carnaby
	Marshall	KW	Sgt	
	Travallion	KJ	Sgt	
	Howard	GF	Sgt	
03.09.44	Brown	AJ	Sgt	Halifax III
	Myers	P	Sgt	LW 475
	Clarke	E	Sgt	LK "K"
	Poulter	KA	Sgt	Landed at Carnaby
	Clark	RH	Sgt	
	Knight	JA	Sgt	
	Gaylor	E	Sgt	
03.09.44	Connop (NZ)	D	F/S	Halifax III
	Williams	WJ	Sgt	LW 473
	Pringle	J	Sgt	LK "I"
	Steels	EA	Sgt	Landed at Carnaby
	Briggs	AG	Sgt	
	Ball	AW	Sgt	
	Burnett (AUS)	WJ	F/S	
03.09.44	Sledge	RG	F/O	Halifax III
	Bouzek (CAN)	JW	F/S	NA 568
	Asker	FW	F/O	LK "Q"
	Fisher	FG	Sgt	Landed at Carnaby
	Atkins	W	Sgt	
	Eplett	F	Sgt	
	Allen	JW	Sgt	

Date	Name	Initials	Rank	Notes
03.09.44	Wilson	W	P/O	Halifax III
	Newman	JG	Sgt	NA 605
	Hull	BE	Sgt	LK "R"
	Leedham	AR	Sgt	Landed at Carnaby
	Rogers	SW	Sgt	
	Revell	HA	Sgt	
	Waller	BH	Sgt	
03.09.44	Wilson	AL	Sgt	Halifax III
	Whitehouse	TS	Sgt	MZ 515
	Hauben	D	Sgt	LK "T"
	Hewitt	DL	Sgt	Landed at Carnaby
	Parsons	TG	Sgt	
	Eaton	R	Sgt	
	Fothergill	RS	Sgt	
03.09.44	Powell	GO	F/O	Halifax III
	Sadler	JE	Sgt	MZ 349
	Bradbury	DW	Sgt	LK"K"
	Toft	JC	Sgt	Landed at Carnaby
	Thornber	J	Sgt	
	Blunstone	F	Sgt	
	Gilbert	E?	Sgt	
09.09.44	Brown	AJ	Sgt	Halifax III
	Myers	P	Sgt	NA 605
	Clarke	E	Sgt	LK "R"
	Poulter	KA	Sgt	landed at Carnaby
	Clark	RH	Sgt	
	Knight	JA	Sgt	
	Gaylor	E	Sgt	
15/16.09.44	Millard	DP	F/S	Halifax III
	Rudd	RD	Sgt	LW 474
	John	WD	F/S	LK"P"
	Noble	GT	Sgt	Landed at Carnaby
	Crawford	AF	Sgt	
	Wyatt	FG	Sgt	
	Fitzgerald	E	Sgt	

Date	Name	Initials	Rank	Notes
07.10.44	Bryson	CW	F/L	Halifax III
	Miles	GA	F/L	MZ 560
	Cuthrie	WA	F/S	LK"C"
	Fahy	F	Sgt	Landed at Carnaby
	Charles	ER	Sgt	
	Grice	J	Sgt	
	Williams	DF	W/O	
14.10.44	Bartrum	RP	P/O	Halifax III
	Johnson	DW	Sgt	MZ 560
	Mathews	JL	Sgt	LK "C"
	Parker	GL	F/S	Landed at Carnaby
	Winter	FI	Sgt	damaged by flak
	Jones	N	Sgt	
	Whelan	HJ	Sgt	
14.10.44	Forrest	AF	F/L	Halifax III
	Skevington	JA	Sgt	NA671
	Hudson	DH	F/O	LK"P"
	Duncan	AC	Sgt	landed at Carnaby
	Anger	AB	F/S	
	Carey	JP	Sgt	
	Tilass	HF	F/S	
23.10.44	Baker (CAN)	WV	F/O	Halifax III
	Johnstone (CAN)	DR	F/O	NA 671
	Harrigan (CAN)	DB	F/O	LK"T"
	Dishart (CAN)	DC	Sgt	Landed at Carnaby
	Inglis	WV	Sgt	
	Brooke CAN)	JR	Sgt	
	Whitaker (CAN)	BL	Sgt	
25.10.44	Howard (CAN)	JW	F/O	Halifax III
	Wilschke (CAN)	CF	F/O	LL 558
	Booth (CAN)	FE	F/O	LK"F"
	Francis (AUS)	AB	F/S	Landed at Carnaby
	Blackmore	FC	F/S	
	McNeal (CAN)	HR	Sgt	
	Jepson (CAN)	HT	Sgt	
	Henham	EC	P/O	

Date	Name	Initials	Rank	Notes
25.10.44	Barton	BB	F/S	Halifax III
	Harrison	LC	Sgt	MZ 559
	Bracewell	JN	Sgt	LK"K"
	Brookes	LA	Sgt	Landed at Carnaby
	Kendall	A	Sgt	
	Grant	CE	Sgt	
	Russ	KA	Sgt	
25.10.44	Wilson	AL	Sgt	Halifax III
	Whitehouse	TS	Sgt	LW 543
	Robertson	D	F/L	LK "S"
	Hewitt	DL	Sgt	Landed at Carnaby
	Parsons	TG	Sgt	
	Eaton	R	Sgt	
	Fothergill	RS	Sgt	
25.10.44	Brown	AJ	Sgt	Halifax III
	Myers	P	Sgt	MA 618
	Clarke	E	Sgt	LK "N"
	Poulter	KA	Sgt	Landed at Carnaby
	Clark	RH	Sgt	Hydraulics u/s, bomb
	Knight	JA	Sgt	doors open
	Gaylor	E	Sgt	
28.10.44	Carabine	RD	F/S	Halifax III
	Perry	HE	F/O	LL 585
	Mills	JR	F/O	LK "R"
	Walker	RD	Sgt	Landed at Carnaby
	Gibb	GD	Sgt	
	Henson	JR	Sgt	
	Blake	P	Sgt	
30.10.44	Marshall	AJ	F/S	Halifax III
	Patton	WF	Sgt	LE 465
	Lawrence	KD	Sgt	LK "F"
	Griffiths	AH	Sgt	Landed at Carnaby
	Elsome	DH	Sgt	
	Tuck	RC	Sgt	
	Thorhley	J	Sgt	

Date	Name	Initials	Rank	Notes
30.10.44	Ewans	TI	F/O	Halifax III
	Rattray	PW	F/S	NA 670
	Owen	IG	F/O	LK "L"
	Bush	WH	F/O	Landed at Carnaby
	Corderby	JC	Sgt	
	Armstrong	KR	Sgt	
	Chester	JH	Sgt	
30.10.44	Aitken	JA	F/S	Halifax III
	Seed	WA	F/S	NA 670
	Carson	JA	F/O	LK "T"
	Stacey	RM	Sgt	Landed at Carnaby
	Thomson	GD	Sgt	
	Boulter	PG	Sgt	
	Naylor	VR	Sgt	
29.11.44	Brown	P	F/L	Halifax III
	McCauley	GT	F/O	NR 193
	Combaz (CAN)	AJ	F/O	LK "V"
	Hunter	WJ	Sgt	Landed at Carnaby
	Grindley	J	Sgt	
	Mann	H	Sgt	
	Freeman	CA	F/S	
24.12.44	Driver	JW	F/L	Halifax III
	McKnight	WJ	P/O	LL 559
	Jellings	EC	P/O	LK "U"
	King	JR	F/S	Landed at Carnaby
	Thompson	I	F/S	
	McCormack	T	F/S	
02.01.45	Gardner	EG	P/O	Halifax III
	Porter	RW	Sgt	LK 830
	Blanche	RJ	Sgt	LK "F"
	Rambert	LM	F/S	Landed at Carnaby
	Sumner	D	Sgt	SI engine oil leak
	Thomas	SA	Sgt	
	White	HB	F/S	

Date	Name	Initials	Rank	Notes
06.01.45	Ingham	RJ	F/O	Halifax III
	Shepley (AUS)	JR	F/S	NA 624
	McLean	DR	F/O	LK "A"
	Welstead	A	Sgt	landed at Carnaby
	Baxter	DG	Sgt	
	Watson	M	Sgt	
	Weaver	DG	Sgt	
	Logan	WT	Sgt	
06.01.45	Donald	DS	F/O	Halifax III
	Giles	W	Sgt	ME 589
	Pegg	R	F/S	LK "S"
	McQueen (AUS)	CN	F/S	landed at Carnaby
	Ballance	G	Sgt	
	Pattison	GR	Sgt	
	Collier	D	F/S	
	Ellis	T	F/S	
13/14.01.45	Carabine	RD	F/S	Halifax III
	Perry	HE	F/O	RG 353
	Mills	JR	F/O	LK "E"
	Earnshaw	N	F/S	landed at Carnaby
	Benson	J	Sgt	
	White?	P	F/S	
	Thomas	SA	Sgt	
16/17.01.45	Ingham	RJ	F/O	Halifax III
	Shepley (AUS)	JR	F/S	landed at Carnaby
	McLean	DR	F/O	
	Welstead	A	Sgt	
	Baxter	DG	Sgt	
	Watson	M	Sgt	
	Weaver	DG	Sgt	
01.02.45	Millard	DP	F/O	Halifax III
	Rudd	HC	Sgt	LW 543
	Long	WJ	P/O	LK "O"
	Cooke	AL	F/S	landed at Carnaby
	Kennedy	HC	Sgt	
	Kemp	RW	F/S	
	Wyatt	RC	F/S	

Date	Name	Initials	Rank	Notes
01.02.45	Wood	D	P/O	Halifax III
	Hudson	RA	Sgt	LL 548
	Penny	NF	P/O	LK "J"
	Saiger	RW	F/O	landed at Carnaby
	Wiltshire	H	F/O	
	Long (CAN)	FJ	F/S	
	Cannon	CA	F/S	
	Holmes	T	W/O	
01.02.45	Brown	P	F/L	Halifax III
	McCauley	GT	F/O	RG 353
	Combaz (CAN)	AJ	F/O	LK "E"
	Hunter	WJ	Sgt	landed at Carnaby
	Grindley	J	Sgt	
	Stone	HA	F/S	
	Freeman	CA	F/S	
02/03.02.45	Shaw	K	P/O	Halifax III
	Hargreaves	PJ	P/O	MZ 988
	Carter	L	F/S	LK "M"
	Barker	HW	F/S	landed at Carnaby
	Relton	K	Sgt	
	Hayes	HT	F/S	
	Palmer	FR	Sgt	
03/04.03.45	Gardner	EG	P/O	Halifax III
	Porter	RW	Sgt	LW 587
	Blanche	RJ	Sgt	LK "A"
	Rambert	LM	F/S	landed at Carnaby
	Sumner	D	Sgt	short of petrol
	Thomas	SA	Sgt	
	White	HB	F/S	
03/04.03.45	Yates	R	F/L	Halifax III
	Bird	TW	F/L	MZ 560
	Decryse	CLF	W/O	LK "C"
	Elder	DC	F/S	landed at Carnaby
	Crawford	AF	Sgt	short of petrol
	Steele	S	F/S	
	Freeman	CAJ	F/S	

Date	Name	Initials	Rank	Notes
11.03.45	Johnson	K	W/O	Halifax III
	Ballsky	M	Sgt	MZ 255
	Hattin (CAN)	VB	F/S	LK "U"
	Carr	PR	Sgt	landed at Carnaby
	Macalpine	CK	Sgt	
	Cochrane	G	Sgt	
	Clifton	CA	Sgt	

617 Squadron

Date	Name	Initials	Rank	Notes
13.03.45	Fauquier (Can)	JE	G/C	
	Ives	CF	F/S	
	Ellwood (Can)	GB	S/L	
	Rumgay	JL	F/L	
	Scannell	JB	F/O	
13.03.45	Cockshott	JV	S/L	
	Pryer	RC	F/S	
	Gosling	LE	W/O	
	Booth	E	P/O	
	Bates	AS	F/S	
	Ford	L	F/S	
	Bradbury	GR	F/S	
13.03.45	Calder	CC	S/L	
	Wakefield	HE	F/C	
	Henison	JH	F/L	
	Crafer	CB	F/L	
	Dale	G	F/O	
13.03.45	Brookes	JF	S/L	
	Short	HR	F/O	
	Jones	JR	F/O	
	Baldwin	EA	F/L	
	Judge	DW	F/L	
	Denwett	RB	P/O	
	Girwan	R	F/L	

Date	Name	Initials	Rank	Notes
13.03.45	Powell	JL	S/L	
	Felton	HW	F/S	
	Bayne	BR	F/L	
	Barron	R	F/O	
	Slater	J	P/O	
	Pengelly	WH	W/O	
	Watson	J	F/O	
13.03.45	McLoughton	JC	F/L	
	Phillips	JD	Sgt	
	Hill	JL	P/O	
	Heath	AL	F/O	
	Ries	OA	W/O	
	Machin	R	F/S	
	Bailey	HR	F/O	
13.03.45	Goodman	LS	F/L	
	Burnett	W	Sgt	
	Watkinson	H	F/O	
	Haywood	HA	F/L	
	Booth	HJ	F/S	
	Hulbert	BS	F/S	
	Lewis	R	Sgt	
13.03.45	Hill (Can)	CN	F/L	
	Sinclaire	A	P/O	
	Murray (Aus)	JD	P/O	
	Kelly	GE	F/O	
	Vaglonini	MR	P/O	
	Dickenson	GW	W/O	
	Forbes	CG	F/O	
13.03.45	Gumley (NZ)	BA	F/L	
	Barnett	EA	P/O	
	Gill	K	P/O	
	Randon	JC	F/L	
	Grimes	SV	F/O	
	Penswick	J	W/O	
	Bell	G	P/O	

Date	Name	Initials	Rank	Notes
13.03.45	Warburton	JC	F/L	
	Coker	JA	Sgt	
	Stanley	BACU	P/O	
	Palmer	PS	F/O	
	Hewitt	KAJ	P/O	
	Lees	CH	F/S	
	Lees	JB	P/O	
13.03.45	Sayers (Aus)	JL	F/L	
	Johnson	VL	F/O	
	Witmer (Aus)	FE	P/O	
	Weaver	EW	P/O	
	Howkins	FE	P/O	
	Vaughan	DH	W/O	
	Barey (Aus)	RP	P/O	
13.03.45	Langley	GW	F/L	
	Bunsell	CE	Sgt	
	Robin	DW	W/O	
	Perry	GL	W/O	
	Saville	JHE	Sgt	
	Jennison	SK	F/O	
	English (Can)	FL	F/O	
13.03.45	Anning	SA	F/L	
	Snedker	FJ	F/S	
	Barleycorn	DH	F/O	
	Valentine	R	F/O	
	Pask (Aus)	M	W/O	
	Neale	M	Sgt	
	Dadge	JA	F/S	
13.03.45	Rawes	DA	F/L	
	Morfitt	JE	Sgt	
	Hodgkinson	J	F/L	
	Roberts	EA	P/O	
	Ross	DE	F/O	
	Bailey	GA	F/S	
	Pain	CW	F/O	

Date	Name	Initials	Rank	Notes
13.03.45	Adams (USA)	W	Lt	
	Swan	A	F/S	
	Collins	TH	P/O	
	Foulkes	RK	F/L	
	Pratt	GR	F/S	
	Scawthorpe	GA	F/S	
	Banning	F	F/S	
13.03.45	Flatman	MB	F/O	
	Ross	RM	Sgt	
	Mackie	G	F/O	
	Kelly	GE	F/O	
	Harwood	AS	F/S	
	Benson	G	W/O	
	Kirk	KC	F/O	
13.03.45	Martin	PH	F/O	
	Bragbrough	J	F/S	
	Jackson	A	W/O	
	Day	DA	F/S	
	Lovatt (Aus)	GN	P/O	
	Mayoh	H	F/S	
	Threbilcock	L	F/S	
13.03.45	Spiers (Aus)	JW	F/O	
	Carrod	AE	Sgt	
	Harrison	JD	F/O	
	Muhl	TG	F/O	
	Warren	IS	W/O	
	Lloyd	NH	F/O	
	Bird	BJD	W/O	
13.03.45	Castagnola	J	F/O	
	Henderson	SJ	F/S	
	Gorringe	FJ	F/T	
	Hebbard (NZ)	L	F/S	
	Broom	DA	F/O	
	Tirel	AD	F/S	
	Ronald	JK	P/O	

Date	Name	Initials	Rank	Notes
13.03.45	Carey (Aus)	DW	F/O	
	Gallagher	A	F/S	
	Fish	CBR	F/S	
	McLennan (Can)	DH	P/O	
	Lamas	AJ	W/O	
	Sharp	AW	F/S	
	Witherick	GA	F/L	

640 Squadron

Date	Name	Initials	Rank	Notes
Aug-44	Bishop	WH	F/Sgt	Halifax III
	Cakebread	FC	Sgt	NA 578 "Q"
	Kane	RA	Sgt	Landed at Carnaby
	Nash	GH	Sgt	
	Gravatte	CH	Sgt	
	Churchill	JE	Sgt	
	Simmonds	EG	Sgt	
Aug-44	Papple	FJ	P/O	Halifax III
	McLean	S	F/S	LK786 "W"
	Hyde	A	F/S	Landed at Carnaby
	Gunstone	RG	Sgt	
	Burns	JW	Sgt	
	Dakin	TW	Sgt	
	McDonald	S	Sgt	
Aug-44	Tily	MJ	F/Sgt	Halifax III
	Goldby	J	F/Lt	LW 641 "J"
	Clare	H	P/O	landed at Carnaby
	Stickens	RJ	W/O	owing to low
	Lowson	R	Sgt	brake pressure
	Bond	AG	W/O	
	Duberley	MM	Sgt	

Date	Name	Initials	Rank	Notes
15.10.44	Fielder	RR	P/O	Halifax III
	Stanley	M	Sgt	MZ308
	Belcher	SA	Sgt	landed at Carnaby
	Woodgate	GH	Sgt	
	Whitton	EJ	F/O	
	Worrall	SP	Sgt	
	Cruickshank	LW	Sgt	
15.10.44	Tily	MJ	F/O	Halifax III
	W-Jones	DD	F/O	MZ939 "M"
	Clare	H	F/L	undercarriage trouble
	Stickens	RJ	W/O	landed at Carnaby
	Lowson	R	Sgt	
	Bond	AG	W/O	
	Duberley	MM	Sgt	
28.12.44	Nicholson	EH	F/O	Halifax III
	Henshaw	D	Sgt	B MZ494
	Watkin	KM	F/S	Landed at Carnaby
	Moore	LH	Sgt	due to hydraulics u/s
	Allen	HT	Sgt	
	Kitching	B	Sgt	
	Clarke	AR	Sgt	
14.01.45	Mundin	OC	F/L	Halifax III
	McKee	E	Sgt	F NR286
	Wright	SE	Sgt	Landed at Carnaby
	Lloyd	FA	Sgt	no brakes
	Campbell	D	F/S	
	Silvester	R	Sgt	
	Hardstaff	T	Sgt	
07.03.45	Buckland	J	F/O	Halifax III
	Gray	AW	F/S	MZ797 U
	Leicht	AA	Sgt	Landed at Carnaby
	Cooney	JH	F/S	Hydraulics u/s
	Goodall	G	Sgt	
	Warman	H	Sgt	
	Martin	WH	Sgt	

Date	Name	Initials	Rank	Notes
07.03.45	Huckle	AW	F/L	Halifax III
	Willoubhey	JB	F/O	NP 958 V
	Walton	WA	F/L	Landed at Carnaby
	McKaig	S	F/S	on 3 engines
	Barrett	M	F/S	
	Allingham	WG	F/S	
	Ralph	WEC	P/O	
24.03.45	Buckland	F	F/O	Halifax III
	Gray	AW	F/S	NR286 F
	Leitch	AA	Sgt	Landed at Carnaby
	Cooney	JH	F/S	Hydraulics u/s
	Goodall	G	Sgt	
	Warman	H	Sgt	
	Martin	WH	Sgt	
11.04.45	Humphrey	FG	W/O	Halifax VI
	Flatley	A	Sgt	NP923 G
	Coxon	R	Sgt	Landed at Carnaby
	Melville	J	Sgt	
	Wharry	W	Sgt	
	Johnson	LM	Sgt	
	Beck	R	Sgt	
11.04.45	Dodd	KM	F/S	Halifax VI
	Russell	AW	Sgt	RG 566 J
	Hendey	HJ	Sgt	Landed at Carnaby
	Palmer	HJ	Sgt	
	Johnson	CW	Sgt	
	Pugh	D	Sgt	
	Carroll	RO	Sgt	
11.04.45	Boonzailer	W	P/O	Halifax VI
	Beaumont	J	Sgt	RG565 K
	White	RE	Sgt	Landed at Carnaby
	Meredith	E	Sgt	
	Mason	J	Sgt	
	Goodwin	E	Sgt	
	Davies	H	F/O	

Date	Name	Initials	Rank	Notes
11.04.45	Tozer	A	F/SL	Halifax VI
	Geake	G	Sgt	RG564 P
	Cowley	JJ	Sgt	Landed at Carnaby
	Beatty	T	Sgt	
	Ford	JG	Sgt	
	Irvine	JS	Sgt	
	Adams	A	Sgt	
11.04.45	Young	CL	F/O	Halifax VI
	Clarkson	D	Sgt	RG588 S
	Reidman	JW	Sgt	Landed at Carnaby
	Scott	A	Sgt	
	Hansard	CW	P/O	
	Slack	GKM	Sgt	
	Melcher	AC	F/S	
11.04.45	Knights	LG	F/S	Halifax VI
	Aikman	RP	Sgt	RG 590 U
	Rothenburg	N	Sgt	Landed at Carnaby
	Collop	CG	Sgt	
	Hogg	AB	Sgt	
	Jones	TH	Sgt	
	Marsham	JC	Sgt	
11.04.45	Barnard	EFE	W/C	Halifax VI
	Johnson	HL	F/S	RG 600 V
	Maguire	DJ	F/O	Landed at Carnaby
	Higgins	WA	Sgt	Aircraft seen to burst
	Smith	AE	Sgt	into flames and hit the
	Clarke	WA	Sgt	ground
	Walton	H	F/O	
11.04.45	Owen	EL	W/O	Halifax VI
	Harris	G	F/O	RG 603 W
	Dutton	H	F/O	Landed at Carnaby
	Trotter	J	Sgt	
	Swain	FJ	Sgt	
	Schwenk	RFJ	Sgt	
	Bateman	BH	Sgt	

141

References

100 Squadron Association archive material
http://www.100squadronassociation.org.uk/index.php/history/history5
[accessed 01.03.15]

158 Squadron Association archive material

Airfield Research Group (1999) Airfield Review No 82

Airfield Research Group (1999) Airfield Review Extra No 85

Airfield Research Group (1994) Airfield Review No 67

Australian Government (2014) Empire Air Training Scheme
http://www.awm.gov.au/encyclopedia.raaf/eats/ [accessed 29.11.14]

Australian Government (2014) http://www.dva.gov.au/aboutDVA/
publications/commemorative/bombercommand/P. [accessed 29.11.14]

East Riding of Yorkshire archive material

Catchpole, B. (1994) Balloons to Bucanneers Yorkshire's role in aviation
since 1785 :

Bomber Command Museum (2014) http://bombercommandmuseum.ca/
bcatp.html [accessed 29.11.14]

British Commonwealth Air Training Programme (2014) http://
www.canadianwings.com/BCATP/ [accessed 29.11.14]

Eden Camp Museum archive material

Falconer, J (1998) Bomber Command Handbook 1939-1945 Sutton
Publishing: Thrupp

Fleet Air Arm Archive (2014) Fleet Air arm and the British
Commonwealth Air Training Plan http://www.fleetairarmarchives.net/
Rollofhonour/TrainingCourses/BCATP_index.html [accessed 29.11.14]

Bomber History http://www.bomberhistory.co.uk/Viaduct/ [accessed
02.03.14] Bielefeld Viaduct

Dambusters http://www.dambusters.org.uk/after-the-dams/raids/bielefeld/
[accessed 02.03.14]

Halpenny, BB (1982) Action Stations 4. Military Airfields of Yorkshire Patrick Stevens: Cambridge

Imperial War Museums archive material

Lincolnshire Aviation Heritage Centre archive information

National Archives Air 2/13870 Deployment Policy for RAF Carnaby

National Archives Air 14/1610 Emergency Runway Carnaby

National Archives Air 24/286 Bomber Command Intelligence Reports

National Archives Air 28/111

National Archives Air 28/125 Carnaby Operations Record Book

National Archives Air 28/1187

National Archives Air 28/1351

National Archives Air 29/710

National Archives Air 29/939

National Archives Works 14/1210

National Archives Air 2 – various squadrons

Rapier, BJ (1980) White Rose Base Air Museum York Publication: York

RAF (2014) http://www.raf.mod.uk/history/ bombercommandno405squadron.cfm [accessed 28.09.14]

RAF (2014) http://www.rafweb.org/Sqn485-490.htm [accessed 05.10.14]

RCAF (2014) http://www.bombercommandmuseum.ca/contribution.html [accessed 05.10.14]

Rhodesia and the RAF (2014) http://rhodesiaandtheraf.blogspot.co.uk [accessed 29.10.14]

Royal New Zealand Air Force (2014) http://www.airforce.mil.nz/about-us/ who-we-are/history/default.htm [accessed 05.10.14]

The National War Museum – New Orleans (2014) http://www.nww2m.com/2012/01/january-26-1942-american-soldiers-arrive-in-great-britain/ [accessed 05.12.14]

Yorkshire Air Museum archive material

Personal memoirs of Gerald Lilley

Personal memoirs of Mr Wade

Williams, G (1995) Flying through fire Grange Books: London

Victoria University (2014) Royal New Zealand Air Force http://nzetc.victoria.ac.nz/tm/scholarly/tei-WH2AirF-c5.html [accessed 30.11.14]

The Eighth Air Force Historical Society http://www.8thafhs.org/combat1944b.htm [accessed 07.12.14]